Archery

FOR BEGINNERS

John C. Williams

with

Glenn Helgeland

UPDATED
AND
REVISED

CONTEMPORARY
BOOKS, INC.
CHICAGO

Copyright © 1976, 1985 by John C. Williams and Glenn Helgeland
All rights reserved
Published by Contemporary Books, Inc.
180 North Michigan Avenue, Chicago, Illinois 60601
Manufactured in the United States of America
Library of Congress Catalog Card Number: 78-72165
International Standard Book Number: 0-8092-5256-2

Published simultaneously in Canada by Beaverbooks, Ltd.
195 Allstate Parkway, Valleywood Business Park
Markham, Ontario L3R 4T8 Canada

contents

The 1972 Olympic archery gold medal won by John Williams.

introduction

I got started in archery the way most kids do. My dad was a bowhunter who branched out into field and target archery. Dad started me shooting when I was eight years old, and I got my first bow for my ninth birthday. Mother had begun shooting, too, because she preferred total family participation to staying home alone. She coached me the first few months, then Dad took over the coaching. He still coaches me when he gets a chance.

He didn't push me; he let me push myself. The more I practiced, the more rapid improvement I made. Improvement hooks people; it hooked me. Then Dad began showing me some of the potential rewards by taking me to archery tournaments. I liked traveling and meeting people and having something special to talk about at school during the week.

Dad early established one credo—"Never go to a tournament unprepared." This means practice. He left me home a couple of times because I wasn't fully prepared. I was shooting well, but I hadn't practiced enough to be in top shape.

Then I got used to the amount of practice required to reach the top and started shooting well enough to win a few times. Winning is always a thrill. But it can also be an endless circle. The more I practiced the better I shot and the

John Williams receiving the archery gold medal at the Olympics.

more I won. And then the more I had to practice to stay there. I won the cadet boys national title at the National Archery Association Championships in 1964 and a year or two later I won the junior boys title.

Then in the spring of 1969, Dad told me he thought I was shooting well enough to try for a place on the United States team to compete in the World Target Championships. At that time my highest FITA Round score was an 1199. (The FITA Round consists of 144 arrows, 36 each at 90, 70, 50, and 30 meters for men's shooting. Perfect score is 1440.) At the tryouts in St. Louis, I shot an 1184 in one day—on what is usually a two-day round. We were staying in a camper, and at 2 A.M. that night we woke up to feel the camper rocking in the wind. The next morning there were tornado and electrical storm warnings. We all shot one end of practice arrows and were then warned off the field. We came back an hour later and shot, without warm-up, two ends at the 90-meter distance. More warnings forced us off the field again, and shortly after we left a bolt of lightning struck the field. We came back and finished the round.

But that bolt of lightning must have been an omen. I didn't break any individual distance records, but when the round was completed I had a 1242 FITA, a world record at that time. When I broke 1200, I broke it good. It was a great psychological lift. I made the United States team as the high-scoring man; I was 15.

At the World Championships, held in Valley Forge, Pennsylvania, Hardy Ward, who had also made the team, shot great, and near the end of a Double FITA was ahead of me by about 15 points. But with only three arrows to go on the 30-meter distance, the last to be shot, the margin was only three points. Hardy's first arrow was a seven. If I could now shoot three tens I would win, because he had had a couple of misses earlier that would have put him second even though our final score would be tied. So I shot a ten. He shot a ten. I shot a ten. He shot a ten. One arrow to go.

I choked and shot a seven and Hardy won the World Championship.

That was the first real pressure I had ever experienced, and it taught me what butterflies in the stomach and pressure really were. One tournament taught me more than I'd learned in three years before that. I realized that, from then on, it was up to me. I could compete on a skill basis; could I do it on a mental basis?

That year I also finished third in the men's division at the NAA National Championships.

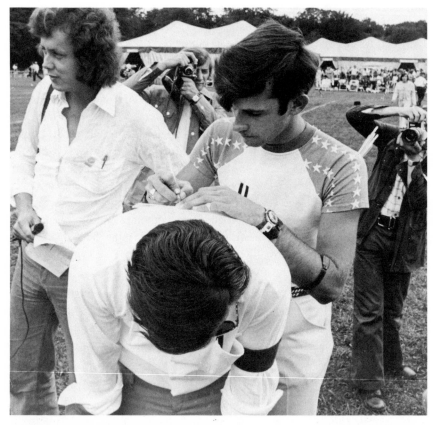

Williams signing autograph after completion of first FITA Round, which set the record at 1268.

In 1970 I didn't shoot much because Dad's company was on strike and we didn't have the money to travel to tournaments.

In 1971, conditions were better and I felt I was ready. I again had the top men's score at the tryouts for the World Championships. At the championships, held in York, England, I was tied for second after the first day, but only one point behind the leader. I made up my mind that if I shot what I wanted to shoot, I could take it. I did, by 67 points, built up over the last 1½ FITA Rounds.

Then I won the NAA National Championships back home a week later. This was only the second time a person had won both the World and National title the same year.

I went into the army right after these tournaments, and my main archery thoughts were simply on making the Olympic team, which was still more than a year away. Making the U.S. Olympic team was the hope and dream of nearly every competitive archer in the country, more so this time because it would be the first official appearance of archery as an Olympic sport.

The night before the Olympic tryouts began, in June, 1972, I fell against the

Williams embraces his mother after the first round of Olympic competition. John's father is behind Mrs. Williams, facing camera.

The target line at 90 meters prior to the opening of competition at the Olympics.

shower head in my room, hooking my shoulder blade on the shower head. I didn't dare tell Dad. He wondered why I wanted to practice early every morning, but I didn't tell him what had happened to my shoulder until the tryouts were completed. I had managed to keep the shoulder from tightening up and won the tryouts.

Then I went into a slump and didn't work my way out of it until the opening day of archery competition in Munich. I had shot 300-350 arrows a day practicing at Munich, trying to work out of the slump. I could feel things falling together the two days before official competition, but I couldn't be positive until competition began.

In other competitive events, I had always been a slow starter. After the first 90-meter end at Munich, on which I had a 51, I watched the scoreboard. They started at the tenth position, working up, and as each name and score went up, I mentally ticked off "I'm ahead of him."

Then my name, the "USA" and the "51" went up on top. I walked back to Dad and asked, "What do I do now?" I was used to chasing someone. He said, "Shoot like you're 20 points behind." So I did, and kept going from there, leading from the first end through the last.

Williams checks his arrows as he walks back to the shooting line.

I shot a world record 1268 FITA on the first round, and came back with a 1260 on the second round. Included in here was a 350 world record score at the 30-meter distance and Double FITA world record score of 2528.

I still don't have an appropriate answer to the question "What was it like?"

When the gold medal was placed around my neck, I felt the most proud of my dad. It was like he was placing that medal on me. He may have worked harder for it, for me, than I did. And that points out the value of good coaching.

Since that day in September of 1972, the Single FITA record has moved from 1268 to an amazing 1341, and the Double FITA has risen to 2571. Part of this improvement is due to advances in equipment technology, but much of it can be traced to improved methods of physical training, mental training, coaching, and technique.

In August of 1973, I signed a professional sports contract with AMF corporation, and from that time to the present I have worked in some aspect of the archery industry. I began coaching about the same time and have developed two Olympians and many world and national champions. Today I am the archery product manager for Yamaha International Corporation and coach of the 1984 United States Olympic archery team.

Archery is a beautiful sport, an ancient and honorable sport. The romance of the ages lives in a drawn bow and the clean, pure flight of an arrow. Archery can be simple, or it can be complex. It can be a backyard relaxation with family and friends, or it can engulf your entire life, as it has mine. Archery is an individualistic sport that will be exactly what you want it to be. Above all, it should be fun.

I began it just as you are now—at the basic beginning, with proper bows, arrows, and accessories, a place to shoot, and the proper instruction.

Your basic equipment needs are very few: a bow, a bowsight, at least half a dozen matched target arrows, a leather armguard, a finger tab, an arrow quiver, and a bow stringer. At little cost, you can learn efficiently. With the right instruction, you'll learn quickly, and have fun while you're learning. Once you have learned the basics, you'll be shooting just like the experts, for they must do exactly the same on each shot that you do. That's the simplicity of archery. After that, as with any sport, the more deeply engrossed you become, the more you discover there is to be explored within the techniques and equipment of archery.

chapter one

equipment

WHAT DO YOU CALL IT; WHAT DOES IT MEAN?

The archery industry, and archers themselves, have worked hard the past few years to develop standardized names and descriptions for the various parts of archery equipment. Some old-time names have been dropped completely, or have simply fallen into disuse. Two prime examples are "fistmele" and "pile."

Fistmele is a 500-year-old term meaning brace height—the distance between the string and the throat of the handle when the bow is braced. It originated because, on the old wooden longbows, the proper brace height was roughly the width of your hand plus the length of your thumb extended at a right angle from your palm. Brace heights on modern bows are much higher, so the term *fistmele* is meaningless today.

Pile is an equally old term meaning target arrow point.

Equipment labeling in crucial areas like bow length and bowstring length used to lack consistency: two bows labeled 62 inches would not be the same length, and two bowstrings labeled 62 inches might fit only one bow, or none.

So in 1968 the Archery Manufacturers Organization (AMO) adopted

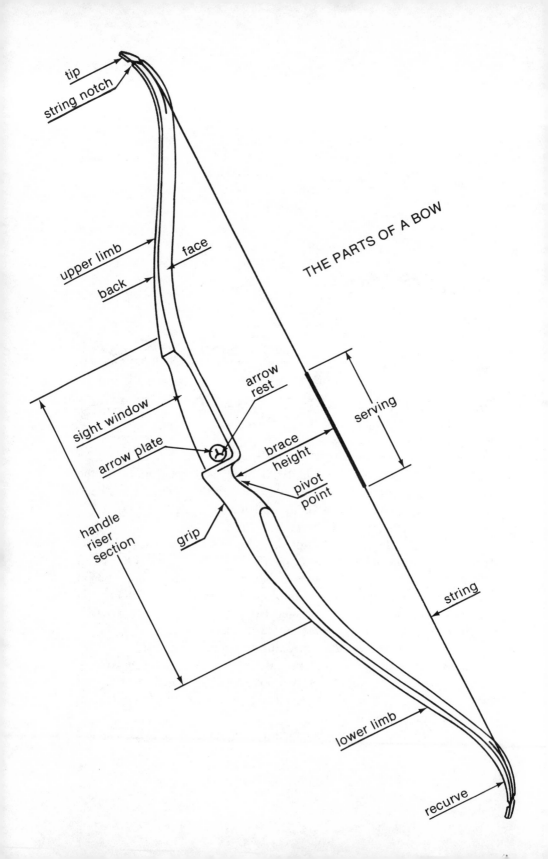

THE PARTS OF A BOW

standardized terminology and standardized lengths for bows and bow-strings, based on a master set of metal cables of defined lengths.

Not all archery manufacturers belong to AMO, but even those who don't have basically adopted the AMO standards.

As the standards become better known, we'll all benefit, because we can walk into an archery shop and buy a 62-inch bowstring that will fit any and all 62-inch bows.

To aid in the acceptance and understanding of the AMO guidelines, we're using their recommended terminology throughout this book.

BOW

The bow is your first purchase. The ideal beginning bow is a *composite* (wood and fiberglass lamination) *working recurve* bow with center-shot design (a sight window cut into the handle). The recurve may be semi-working or fully working; the latter gives the most cast and smoothness. It will be similar in design and shooting characteristics to the more highly refined bows you'll move up to as you increase your shooting skill, yet a good beginning bow of this style will cost only $40–$60. As with all archery equipment, buy the best bow you can afford; you'll get better performance and be more satisfied with it.

Bows range anywhere from about 48 inches to 70 inches in length. Shorter length bows are hunting bows, and longer bows are usually target bows (this is explained more fully later in this chapter). And they vary in draw weight (the pounds of force needed to draw a bow a certain distance) from almost zero for training bows to over 100 pounds. Standard production bows, however, run 20 to 70 pounds. Most hunting weights are 45 pounds or above, with around 40 pounds considered the practical minimum. Target bow draw weights range from 10 to 50 pounds, with the 40-50 pound draw weights used primarily in field archery and longer outdoor target distances.

Under AMO standards, bow weights are marked for the number of pounds of energy needed to draw the bow to 28 inches. You will note this marking at the base of the lower limb on the facing of the bow. It will say, for example, 30# @ 28'', or whatever the draw weight actually is for that bow.

A rule of thumb for selecting target archery bows:

Boys and girls 8-10 years —10 to 15 pounds draw weight
Boys and girls 11-15 years —15 to 25 pounds draw weight
Girls above 16 and women—20 to 35 pounds draw weight
Boys above 16 and men —30 pounds and up draw weight

You must remember that the draw weights given here are that weight at 28 inches of draw. If your draw length is not 28 inches, you will have to adjust accordingly, for with each additional inch of draw length above 28 inches you will be adding 2-2½ pounds of draw weight, and for each inch below 28 inches you must subtract 2-2½ pounds. This is very important, for you must have arrows that match your bow weight *at your draw length.*

For instance, if your draw length is 30 inches, you would actually be drawing four to five additional pounds; thus, you would be drawing 30 pounds on a bow marked for 25 pounds at 28 inches. And if your draw length is only 26 inches, you would be drawing only 20 pounds on a bow marked 25 pounds at 28 inches.

The most common mistake archers make when choosing a bow is to buy one with too heavy a draw weight. The buyer will select a bow that appeals to him, draw it once—and probably shake like a leaf in an October wind while doing so—but then pronounce "that's for me" if he manages to get it to full draw.

Part of this mistake is caused by ego ("I'm not a weakling!") and part by lack of knowledge. The proper draw weight bow for you is one that you can draw several times, hold comfortably at full draw for five seconds or so, *and shoot accurately.* You may be able to draw and hold a certain draw weight, but if you cannot shoot that bow accurately, go to a lighter weight.

Be realistic. You must be able to handle the bow properly—it's not supposed to handle you. You must have a light enough bow that you can work with it easily as you practice countless shots to develop your shooting form and skills. It is far better to choose a bow that may seem a little light, and then go to a heavier bow as your skills and strength develop, than it is to start with the maximum bow you can handle. You are not seeking a physical battle, you are seeking a streamlined, coordinated effort. Leave the battling to the wrestlers.

Proper bow length is also important. Many people, on first viewing a selection of bows, view a short bow as a sweet and sexy thing. It may be —if the archer is also short, sweet, and sexy. Or at least short and sexy.

A short person would handle a short bow more easily than a longer bow. He/she would not be troubled by the angle of the string on his/her fingers at full draw because the draw length would probably be less than 28 inches and the angle of the string would thus not be overly acute.

But put that short bow in the hands of a tall, long-armed archer, and that archer will severely pinch his draw hand fingers upon full draw. The angle of the string would be far too acute.

Target bows for men are usually 66-70 inches long; for women and young people, 62-66 inches. Hunting bows generally fall in the 52''-62'' range, because the longer bows would be cumbersome in the forest.

Bowstring

Nearly all bowstrings today are made of Dacron. It stretches very little and lasts a long time. Recently, a new material called Kevlar has come on the scene. It has almost no stretch and is much stronger than Dacron, but it also costs more and does not last quite as long.

Manufacturers have determined the most efficient brace heights for the various bows they produce. Accept the manufacturer's suggested brace height for your bow until you have shot it enough to determine whether a little more or a little less brace height would help that bow perform more efficiently for your shooting style. To increase brace height slightly, twist the string *in the direction the serving was applied*. This will shorten the string slightly. To decrease brace height, unwind the string a few turns, but never go back beyond the zero twist installed by the manufacturer. Doing so will loosen the serving and weaken the string.

A string should never have more than 10 twists; above this point, friction in the strands is too high and the string may break easily.

Strings manufactured under AMO specifications are built in one-inch increments and marked for the proper draw weight bow they should be used upon. An AMO standard 66-inch string will fit an AMO standard 66-inch bow.

Lighter bows most efficiently use a string with fewer strands; heavier draw weight bows need more strands in the string to withstand the increased pressure.

Standard recommendations are: 20-30 pound bow, 8 strands; 25-35 pound bow, 10 strands; 35-45 pound bow, 12 strands; 45-55 pound bow, 14 strands; 55-80 pound bow, 16 strands.

These guidelines are not the absolute, final gospel. For instance, some archers may wish to use a 10-strand string on a 35-pound bow because the string will have less weight and air resistance, and will thus allow the bow to recover faster from full draw. This allows the archer to shoot the arrow a few more yards than with the recommended 12-strand string. Obviously, the lighter string will be under extra pressure and will probably break or fray sooner.

Beginning archers should start out with bowstrings of Dacron because of its durability and other forgiving characteristics. It also costs much less. For the past several years, top archers have been using bowstrings made of Kevlar, a manmade fiber stronger and lighter than steel of equivalent strands. Although Kevlar is more critical, the properties of lightness and low stretch as compared with Dacron are an advantage to top shooters.

The bowstring should have no more serving than necessary to protect the Dacron from friction at the loops and at the drawing finger positions. Usual serving length is 4-5 inches at the loops and 8-10 inches at the finger position.

Most strings are served with nylon. Monofilament is the other common serving material. It does not fray like nylon, but if it is not glued properly in a couple of extra spots, it will unwind faster than you can blink when it breaks.

You will note that the loops at the ends of the string are not the same size. The larger loop fits over the upper limb; the smaller loop over the lower limb. When you unbrace the bow, the large loop will slide down over the limb. You can hold the lower loop in place with a commercial tip protector or a rubber band.

A bare bowstring is not ready to shoot. You must first mark a nocking point location slightly above 90° on a horizontal plane from

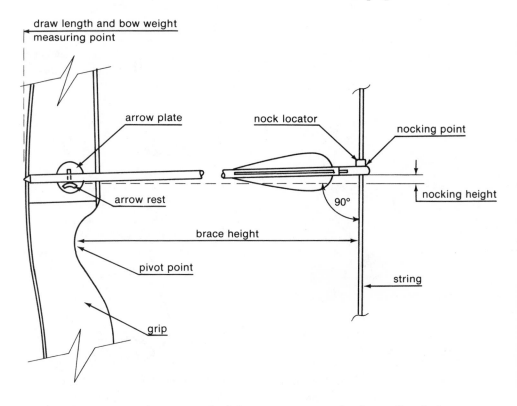

the arrow rest. A commerical bow square works best, for it has fractional-inch increments marked on the square and you can be exactly sure of the proper location every time you attach a new nocking point.

There are several versions of commercial nocking points available. Some clamp on the string with a pliers, others are small tubes of rubber that must be slipped into position over the bowstring loops, and still others are small loops of plastic that constrict firmly in place when you heat them. You can also use dental floss, winding it around the bowstring serving serving several times until a suitable bulk is built up. A dab of clear lacquer will cement the floss in place.

When determining the proper nocking point location, archers prefer to first mark a tentative location with a pen or grease pencil on the string serving for test shooting. Then, when the proper height is closely determined, they attach the nocking point locator and make whatever minor adjustments up or down are needed.

THREE TYPES OF ARROW REST

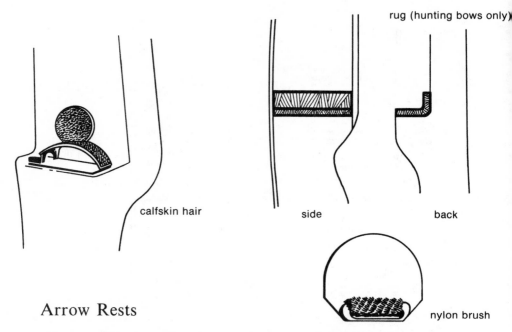

calfskin hair   side   back

rug (hunting bows only)

nylon brush

Arrow Rests

The arrow rest should support the arrow before the shot, but it should not cause any drag upon the arrow when it is shot. When the bow is properly set up and tuned, the arrow should jump slightly up and to the side from the arrow rest upon the shot.

Less expensive target and hunting bows are usually equipped with a strip of rug-like material or soft bristle glued to the entire bow shelf. This type of rest obviously gives firm support, but because of its length, can also cause drag on the arrow. In addition, constant use can wear or depress a groove in the material.

A finger-type or horizontal bristle rest works better, especailly the finger-type rest. These are made of plastic or plastic-coated wire. They will "give" slightly under pressure of the arrow, but will hold the arrow securely in place without impeding its forward motion, and generally last a long time.

The arrow plate that attaches to the bow window and provides a side contact point for the arrow is made of leather or a short bristle material.

Arrow rests and plates attach adhesively to the bow.

ARROWS

Arrows are made of wood (Port Oxford cedar), fiberglass, and aluminum. Wood is by far the least expensive, so most archers begin with wooden arrows. However, wooden shafts are less durable and can warp. A dozen wooden arrows, depending on quality, will cost $8–$30. Fiberglass arrows are tough and flexible; they last a long time. They are also more uniform than wood. They cost 1½ to two times what wooden arrows cost. This initial cost is usually offset by longevity. Aluminum arrows are the most uniform, arrow to arrow, and are light and strong. Serious target archers use aluminum arrows almost exclusively. They can be straightened when bent, and if not bent beyond repair will last indefinitely. They also cost $25–$75 a dozen.

The fiberglass-graphite arrows are relatively new and are used almost exclusively by bowhunters. The shafts are light, tough and very consistent in construction from arrow to arrow. They cost roughly the same as aluminum arrows. Easton Aluminum has recently developed a carbon fiber-wrapped aluminum arrow shaft with about 70% of the diameter and weight of a comparable aluminum arrow. There is about a 10% gain in arrow speed. This shaft is like the Rolls Royce—not everybody drives them. This shaft is only for top archers. Cost is $180–$200 for a set of 10 shafts.

Aluminum and fiberglass arrows, plus the fiberglass-graphite and carbon-aluminum arrows, are hollow. The only exceptions are the fiberglass and metal fishing arrow, which are solid to provide the needed momentum for water penetration.

Always be sure your arrows are matched in spine (shaft stiffness) to

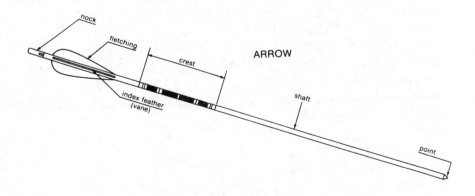

your bow weight *at your draw length,* and are cut to the proper length. (The raw shaft is supplied 32 inches long.)

The average adult man will use a 28-inch arrow. The average adult woman and teenager will use a 26-inch arrow. The average subteen will use a 24-inch arrow.

You can determine your proper arrow length in two ways:

1. Most archery shops have a very light bow with a long arrow marked in one-inch increments. Draw this bow just as you would a regular bow, and come to your proper anchor. The shopkeeper will check this length (usually after you draw several times to establish an average for him—you won't consistently draw to the same length at the beginning). You can then have your arrows cut to the proper length. They may be slightly longer, and still perform well; but they can never be used when they're cut too short for your draw length. A too-short arrow is dangerous—it could hang up on the arrow rest, or strike the bow on release, or puncture your bow hand.

2. Place an arrow nock in the middle of your chest, with your arms extended and palms together. The arrow point will protrude past your fingertips. For proper length, the point of the arrow should extend at least half an inch past your fingertips.

Wooden arrows are generally spined for 10-pound ranges, i.e., 25–35 pounds, 35–45 pounds, 45–55 pounds, etc. Fiberglass arrows are marked on a stiffness scale of 1–12, with #1 arrows being lightest spined (least stiff) and #12 arrows heaviest spined. Aluminum arrows are marked in two ways: (1) a series of four numbers that indicate shaft diameter and wall thickness, ranging from 1314 to 2219 and (2) a three-digit series of magnum numbers from .308 to .328. In both instances, higher numbers indicate heavier spine. In the four-digit numbering system, the first two numbers indicate the outside diameter of the shaft in 64ths of an inch and the latter two numbers indicate the shaft wall thickness in 1000ths of an inch.

If your draw weight and draw length indicate an arrow stiffness that falls right on the borderline between two sizes, you would be wise to choose the heavier-spined arrow. There are many things you can do with your bow to make it shoot a heavier-spined arrow properly, but not a lighter-spined arrow.

Nocks

Arrow nocks are available in two basic types—straight inner line, and snap-on. The straight inner line nocks are of two types—the basic "speed" nock, with straight outer lines and a small ridge on the outer surface that corresponds to the cock feather so you can properly nock the arrow on the string without looking at it, and the smaller, tapered-outer-edge nocks that many serious target archers use. The smaller nock presents less opportunity for your fingers inadvertently to pinch the nock and restrict arrow flight.

The snap-on nocks have a slightly smaller groove than the other nocks, and then have an enlarged circle at the base of the groove in which the string is seated. The outer diameter is flattened somewhat to fit better between the fingers. The snap-on type is better able to hold your arrow on the string should you move your string fingers.

Most beginning arrows are equipped with speed nocks.

NOCKS

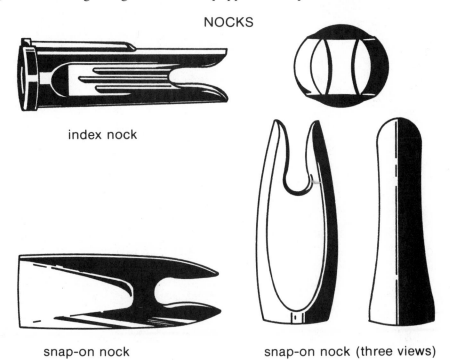

index nock

snap-on nock   snap-on nock (three views)

Fletching

Feathers are by far the most commonly used fletching material. They are inexpensive, easy to affix, and last a long time. They are available in left-wing and right-wing style. Left-hand shooters should use left-wing feathers and right-hand shooters should use right-wing feathers. Since the way an arrow spins depends on whether the shooter is right- or left-handed, and feathers are rough on one side and smooth on the other, the wing side must match the shooting side for best performance.

Many serious target archers, and some hunters, now use molded rubber or plastic vanes instead of feathers. Vanes are not affected by wet weather, and they often permit finer tuning of equipment.

Most arrows carry three fletches—two hen fletches, the outer edges of which align vertically with the bow's sight window and string when the arrow is properly nocked, and a cock feather, which sits at right angles to the sight window. Arrows can also be outfitted with four fletches, either on a 75°/105° arrangement or a consistent 90° setup. The theory is that with four fletches, physically smaller fletches can be used that will have the same stabilizing effect on the arrow as three larger fletches, yet the archer will have less trouble with fletches striking the arrow rest or sight window as they fly by. Also—and this is most commonly a concern of bowhunters—in the excitement of nocking an arrow and shooting, with a four-fletch arrangement your arrow will be properly nocked whichever way you place it on the bowstring. Thus, you can keep your eyes on the game and not need to look at your bowstring to be sure the arrow is nocked properly.

Arrows can be fletched straight, spiral, or helical. Straight fletching is affixed parallel to the shaft. Spiral is offset two or three degrees, but the fletch remains straight with itself. Helical is offset the same degree, but a slight twist is imparted to the fletch, which theoretically helps it stabilize the arrow better.

The fourth type of fletching is the flu-flu: Either one uncut feather is wound around the shaft, or several uncut feathers are positioned like normal fletching. Both systems allow the arrow to fly swiftly for 50-60 yards; then the extra size and/or shape of the fletching produces such

ARROW FLETCHING

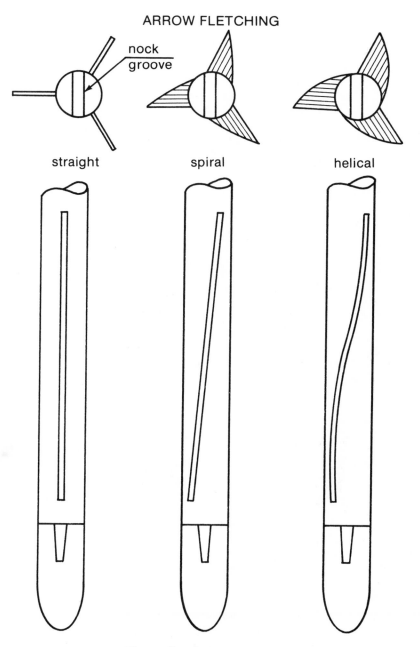

nock
groove

straight   spiral   helical

Three-fletch arrows have
the fletching applied
120° from each other

Four-fletch arrows have
the fletching applied either
90° from each other or 75°/105°

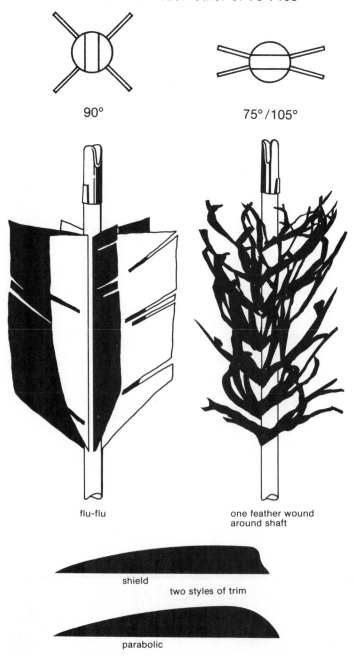

90°

75°/105°

flu-flu

one feather wound
around shaft

shield

two styles of trim

parabolic

an air drag that the arrow falls swiftly, almost seeming to die in midair. This arrow is commonly shot at hand-thrown targets or flying birds.

Fletches will have a parabolic or straight cut at the rear. All target arrows are fletched with the parabolic cut, for this style allows less vacuum to develop directly behind the fletch. The vacuum that develops behind the straight cut increases drag and also causes the rear part of the feather to lie down in flight, which decreases its stabilizing ability.

Points

There are six basic point types—target, field, broadhead, blunt, fish, and bird. The target point is small and light. The field point is heavier and longer, generally matching the grain weight of the broadheads you will be shooting during hunting season. Broadheads are usually three-bladed or four-bladed; there are, however, two-bladed and six-bladed heads available. Years ago, two-bladed heads predominated, but they

ARROW POINTS

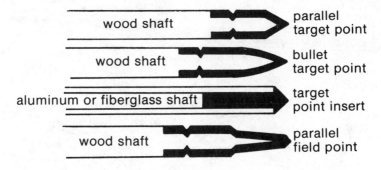

BROADHEADS

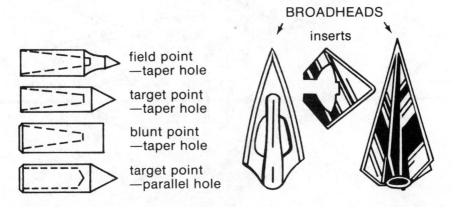

were judged not as efficient for their purpose as multi-bladed heads. Blunts, which are flat-tipped, are heavy and are used for plinking and small game hunting. Bird heads are generally unearthly looking arrangements, usually employing wire loops to provide a larger striking surface. Fish points are solid metal and barbed; the point either screws off or the barbs retract to remove the fish.

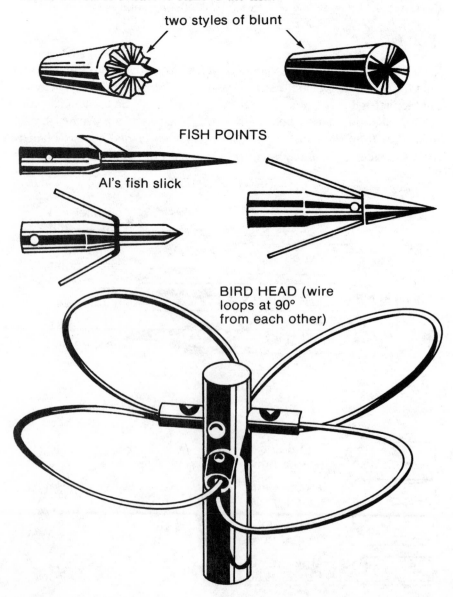

two styles of blunt

FISH POINTS

Al's fish slick

BIRD HEAD (wire loops at 90° from each other)

ACCESSORIES

Armguards

Armguards do just what they say they do, for to strike a bare bow arm with a bowstring is a painful, and never forgotten, experience. Armguards also hold sleeves snugly, keeping the material out of the way of the bowstring upon release.

Armguards can be short, covering your bow arm from just back of the wrist to just short of your elbow, or they can be long, extending from just back of your wrist to considerably above your elbow. The shorter armguards are most used by target archers; the longer armguards by hunters. They must be thick enough to protect, but still be flexible enough to fit your arm. Attachment straps should be adjustable to allow for varying arm sizes.

TYPES OF ARMGUARDS

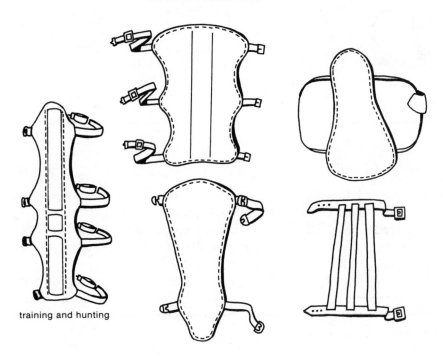

training and hunting

Finger Tabs and Gloves

These protect fingers and give a smoother release. Tabs are most often made of leather, but are also made of plastic. They are available in several shapes and sizes, and in double layer and single layer styles. Obviously, the double layer styles give the most protection; if you shoot a heavy draw weight, the double layer will work best. Tabs are most popular because they can be trimmed to size; the most common mistake is using a tab too large. Most are too long; trim them so they will just cover your bent fingers in drawing position. Also trim those that are too wide.

Shooting gloves, with stalls for the first three fingers, are used almost exclusively by bowhunters. They are usually made of heavier leather. Some hunters find them more comfortable to wear and faster to use.

TYPES OF FINGER PROTECTION

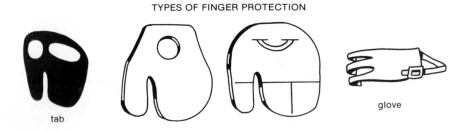

tab   glove

Sling (optional)

A finger or bow sling is not necessary when you're beginning, but you will undoubtedly find it helpful as you progress in skill. The bow sling is affixed to your bow handle riser just below your bow hand, and has a loop that fits loosely over your wrist. The finger sling simply fastens over thumb and forefinger of your bow hand.

The purpose of this accessory is to permit you to shoot the bow with a loose grip. The sling holds the bow safely in your hand upon release, and you're less likely to twist or torque the bow as you shoot. This, of course, produces a better shot.

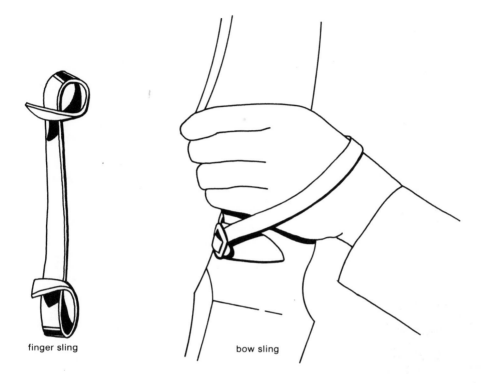

finger sling   bow sling

Quivers

Belt quivers, which simply clip on, are universally used by target archers. They should be deep enough and large enough in inside diameter to prevent your arrows from falling out as you move and to allow easy arrow removal. Fletching also suffers if the quiver is jammed with arrows.

Ground quivers are also used. Some hold only arrows, some also hold your bow.

Bowhunters generally use bow quivers, which fasten directly to the bow, but they also use hip quivers or back quivers. They are available in several sizes and styles, and each style has its adherents.

TYPES OF QUIVERS

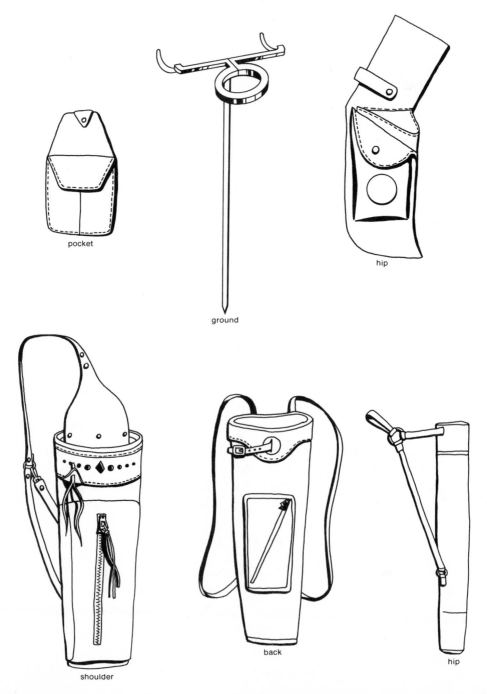

pocket

ground

hip

shoulder

back

hip

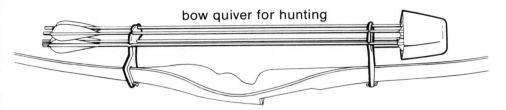

bow quiver for hunting

Stabilizers

Serious target archers have found the stabilizer to be a boon to their scores. The stabilizer is nothing more than a metal rod extending from the back of the bow with a metal weight on the end of the rod. Some archers use more than one stabilizer; in fact, the number of stabilizers, and the length and weight of each, are continually discussed, for each archer has a personal preference as to which setup works best for him/her.

The added weight reduces bow arm movement, which improves the shot. It also makes the bow turn or torque more slowly in your hand upon release (if torquing is your problem). Thus, the arrow has cleared the bow before it can be affected by the torque.

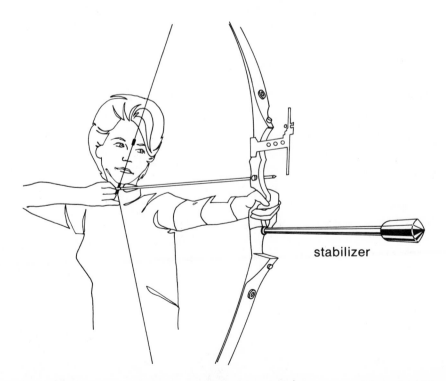

stabilizer

Stabilizers can be from a few inches to a few feet in length. Some are solidly screwed into the back of the bow; others have couplers that permit a slight movement. Some have weights that can be slid forward or backward on the rod.

The best stabilizer system is the one that helps the archer shoot his best. Obviously, it is not the same for everyone.

You will not embark upon the stabilizer road until you have become quite skilled in the basics of archery; stabilizers provide an advantage only in the hands of skilled archers with top-flight equipment.

Bowsights

A bowsight definitely helps your aim, although many bowhunters prefer not to use them, saying the sight only slows them down.

Sights can be very basic, with only a single marking pin, or they can be quite extravagant, with levels and extensions and hoods and minute adjustments.

But they all help you correct your aim horizontally and vertically. Whether you mount the sight on the back or the face of the bow is a personal choice. Those who prefer it on the back believe they have a better view of the sight because it is farther from their eye, that it allows more critical aiming because the aiming dot is relatively smaller in reference to the target center. Those who prefer to have their sight on the face of the bow are concerned about accurate shooting at long yardages, for the closer position allows proper vertical setting of the sight pin without interfering with the arrow or sight window.

Most high quality target sights have some arrangement based around an aiming dot inside a circular frame and/or hood. Some archers remove the pin and use only the hood. Less expensive sights simply have open pins, either singly or in multiples. Bowhunting sights also have rangefinder styles, which permit you to fit the image of the target within a predetermined frame size. Proper fitting of target size to rangefinder frame setting means the bowhunter is on target.

High quality target sights usually also have a level, or bubble, as it is also called, as an integral part of the sight unit. This helps solve bow canting problems.

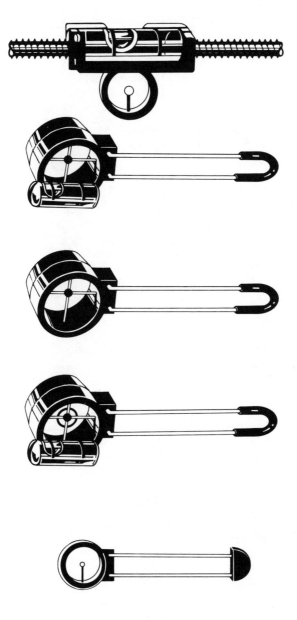

sight apertures

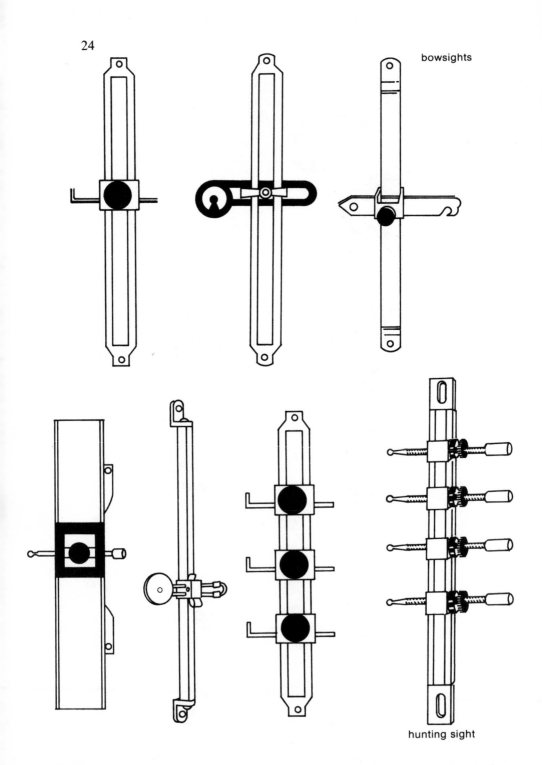

24

bowsights

hunting sight

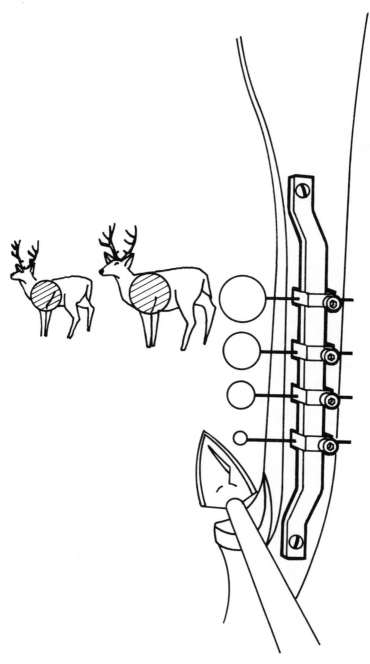

rangefinder bowsight

TARGETS AND STANDS

Target matts are made of excelsior or marsh grass. Taken care of, they can last a long time. Grass is burlap-covered. Excelsior is generally paper-covered. Target butts can be made of several layers of corrugated cardboard pressed together and tied, or of straw or hay bales. If you plan to use corrugated cardboard, lay the cardboard flat so you will be shooting into the corrugations from their ends, and always shoot straight into them. If you shoot from an angle, a corrugation could catch an aluminum arrow and bend it. If you are using straw or hay bales, always shoot into the sides of the bales. The arrows will pull out much easier when shot parallel to the stems of the material. You can also use circular foam targets, which are roughly four feet in diameter and 10''-12'' thick.

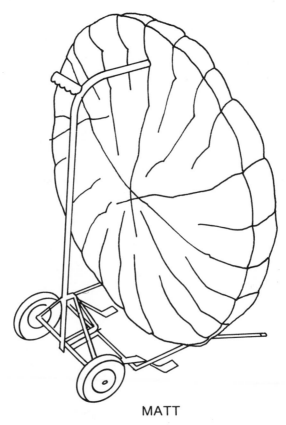

MATT

Hunters, when practicing with broadheads, will either build a back-stop and fill it with clean sand, or dig a shallow pit and pile the removed sand just behind the pit. Broadheads must *never* be shot into the standard target matt or butt material because the sharp edges will cut the material to shreds.

Excelsior, marsh grass, and straw or hay bales must be supported in some manner. You can build an easel like the one shown here to support the excelsior or marsh grass matts. These will not blow over in the wind, and a loop of cord fastened to the matt and dropped over the top of the easel will hold the matt securely. Commercial stands are available for the smaller matt sizes.

Bales of straw or hay can be pinioned between two upright posts, or set on a heavier easel that provides the necessary base and back support. Since bales are much heavier than matts, either place them in a permanent position (and cover them with a sheet of plastic when not in use) or attach strong wheels to the base of the easel.

Rain can damage excelsior and marsh grass matts, so store them in a protected dry place when not in use.

Whichever target style is used, be sure it cannot tip forward. A host of broken or bent arrows is an expensive sight to behold.

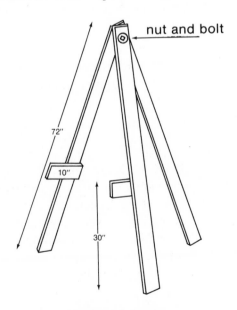

TRIPOD EASEL

HOW THE BOW AND ARROW WORK

Old-time photos—and even some photos from not too long ago—show the traditional wooden longbow in use. Wood was the best material available; it produced bows that shot smoothly and reasonably accurately. But weather was a bugaboo: wooden bows took a "set" (the wood remained in a strung position when the string pressure was released, so the springiness that produced the strength to shoot an arrow was lost), they lost cast on hot days, became brittle on cold days, and warped when wet.

The invention of fiberglass solved some of these problems. Fiberglass is strong and long-wearing, impervious to weather, and inexpensive. Bows molded from solid fiberglass were durable, and almost anyone could buy one. They had better cast than wood bows; but they were still not capable of the speed desired, and they vibrated or "kicked" in your hand upon release. They were also heavy.

However, since they are inexpensive and durable, many schools and camps still prefer to use solid fiberglass bows.

A combination of fiberglass and wood, taking the strengths of each and hopefully discarding the disadvantages of each, proved to be a major jump forward. These are the composite bows of today, some of which now also include metal handles to go with wood/fiberglass limbs.

Wood in the handle and the core of the limbs provided lightness and smooth shooting. Thin strips of fiberglass cemented on the backing and facing of the limbs provided strength, durability, and shooting speed.

New designs brought the bow to further advancement. This included deflexed limbs, reflexed limbs (which increased cast by bending away from the direction of the string draw), then the static (or nonworking) recurve, the short-working recurve, and finally the full-working recurve. These were all developed to add more cast, smoother draw, and reduced stack. (Stack is the sudden, intense buildup of resistance as you get near full draw.) This also included the development of the sight window, a section cut out of the handle just above the grip, in which the arrow rest and bowsight can be positioned.

Where previously, in wood or fiberglass, such a cutting into the bow

TYPES OF BOWS

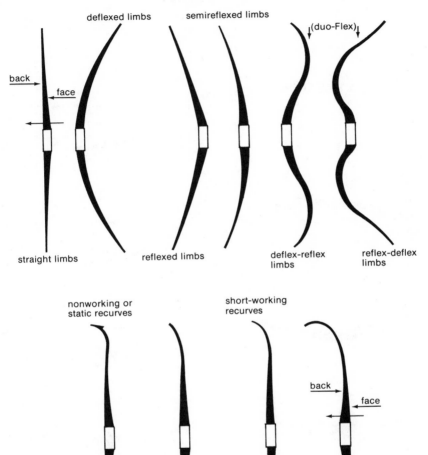

deflexed limbs

semireflexed limbs

(duo-Flex)

back

face

straight limbs

reflexed limbs

deflex-reflex
limbs

reflex-deflex
limbs

nonworking or
static recurves

short-working
recurves

back

face

semiworking
recurved limbs

long-working
recurves

handle riser section would have weakened the bow beyond efficient use, the new design of wood, or wood/fiberglass laminate, permitted

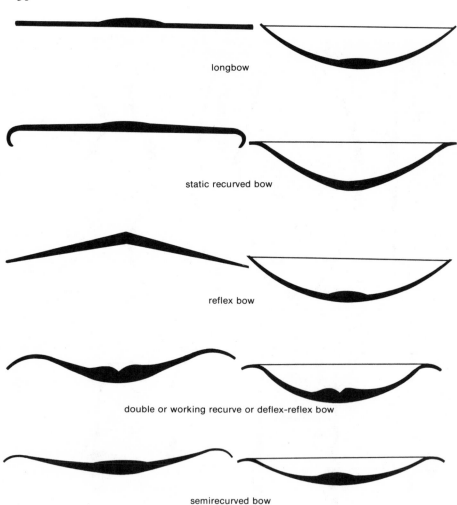

longbow

static recurved bow

reflex bow

double or working recurve or deflex-reflex bow

semirecurved bow

this cutting. This strength allowed a shaped grip section to be cut into the handle—as opposed to the old ''broomstick'' feel of wooden long-bows or solid fiberglass bows, and also provided the strength through the narrow section remaining after the sight window had been cut.

This cutout also began solving an age-old problem—shooting *around* the bow. Previous bows, without the cutout, prevented the shooter from pointing the arrow directly at the target. Instead, it rested alongside the thick handle and pointed slightly off to the side. This meant that arrows were driven off center as the string force moved directly forward. The arrow would need to bend several times in flight (arrow paradox) before straightening out into true flight.

The system was stable *if* arrows were matched perfectly and spined exactly for the individual bow being shot.

With the development of the cutout principle, and the resulting near center-shot and full center-shot bows, the arrow could be pointed directly at, or almost directly at, the target. This increased accuracy and reduced the bending action of the arrow upon release. All arrows shot in all bows bend to a certain degree, simply from the force of the string driving it suddenly forward; however, the less it bends before straightening into true flight, the easier it is to shoot, the faster and more efficiently it will fly.

However, a bow cannot be efficiently cut much beyond center shot because the arrow still needs guidance upon release from some point other than the forward force of the string. The arrow plate or side pressure point does this.

The working recurve, which allows two to five inches of the string at each limb tip to actually touch the recurve as it moves forward on release, added much more stability to bows while maintaining increased cast.

The ''working'' recurve means that all parts of the limb are storing energy as the bow is drawn. Stresses are also distributed more evenly over the limb, and lighter, thinner handles and limbs can thus be made in the fiberglass/wood composites, which are not as cumbersome as older bows. Performance is better, because the working recurve has more energy stored early in the draw, and as the archer comes closer to full draw the string will leave physical contact with the recurves and the bow will, in effect, have a longer length (tip to tip) over which to draw. A long bow is generally easier to draw than a short bow because there's more distance to spread the stress over. Thus, it will also draw smoother with less stack.

Upon release, the string starts forward more slowly from the working recurve bow. But as the string again makes contact with the recurve, those parts of the string touching the recurve aren't moving any more. In effect, a shorter string is then being used and the string accelerates smoothly. This smoothness causes stability and cast.

There is a great variability in lengths and designs of recurve bows, for several reasons. Some archers need speed and cast (in long-range field and target shooting or hunting) and thus are willing to sacrifice a certain degree of stability. Other archers prefer stability and smooth draw (for target shooting at fixed, close distances), so they won't be overly concerned with speed. They will rarely shoot bows shorter than 64 inches, usually 68 to 70 inches. Bowhunters, on the other hand, rarely use bows longer than 64 inches. They are concerned with speed; but a shorter, physically lighter (mass weight) bow is also much easier to carry and hold over long periods of time when hunting. They will not want a bow that stacks unduly, because they use much heavier draw weights if they are capable of handling them (40–45 pounds is about average for women, 60 pounds for men. The heavier draw weights, teamed with heavier hunting arrows, provide better penetration in big game animals.) They will want a practical smoothness in a bow, but they won't be as highly concerned with stability as the target archer because they must rely on getting their first (and usually only) shot to the proper target. They do not need the stability that the target archer requires for an afternoon of shooting at several targets where the last arrow counts just as much as the first arrow, but no more than the first arrow.

The one-piece recurve bow has a brother—the takedown recurve, a three piece unit with the limbs detaching from the handle riser.

Takedowns were designed for multiple use. The archer could use a light draw weight set of limbs for target shooting and a heavier set for bow hunting. One handle riser section will work in both circumstances; thus the archer has two bows but has had to buy only a second set of limbs, not an entire new bow. So he's saved some money.

And if the archer wants to try limbs of different weights from those he is now using, he has only to buy the new limbs, not an entire bow.

There are also recurve bows now available with adjustable poundages.

The takedown bow (in its collapsed state) is much less bulky and thus easier to store and carry than the traditional long one-piece bow.

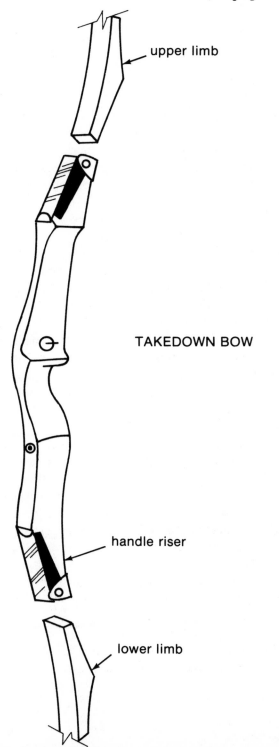

upper limb

TAKEDOWN BOW

handle riser

lower limb

Competitive archers and bowhunters who travel appreciate this compactness.

Compound Bows

This is the most popular bow style used today in the United States. It is used primarily by bowhunters and field archers. The compound bow and two recent variations on its theme—the cam bow and the dynabow—are not legal for international target competition, although they are used in certain international field archery competitions but not all.

Through a system of cables and an eccentric (off-center) pulley attached at each limb tip, this bow generally stores more energy in the limbs than does a recurve bow, and also draws much differently. Because the eccentric pulleys turn over on an axle in mid-draw, peak resistance is reached early in the draw. Once this peak of resistance is reached, the remainder of the draw is much easier. Thus, a 45-pound draw weight compound bow reaches 45 pounds of resistance at or before mid-draw, yet at full draw the archer will be holding only 23 to 35 pounds. On release, this works in reverse, with the eccentrics providing the full 45 pounds of energy as they turn forward. Compounds generally have a letoff of 30% to 50%, although some have as little as 20%.

Early compound bows were called four-wheelers, because they had two eccentric pulleys on limb tips and two center-mounted pulleys attached to the middle of each limb. Most compounds today have only the eccentric pulleys and are called two-wheelers. Two-wheelers generally have the most letoff, while four-wheelers have the least.

Cam bows have an egg-shaped cam instead of a round eccentrically-mounted wheel at the limb tip. They generally are able to store more energy than other compounds, but they also can be a bit more difficult to shoot well.

Dynabows have a cam arrangement on the lower limb tip but no eccentric of any kind on the upper limb tip. The string is attached to the limb.

The compound principle was quickly accepted by bowhunters for it permitted the person who formerly shot a 45-pound recurve bow, for instance, to shoot a 55- to 60-pound compound, yet hold 45 pounds or

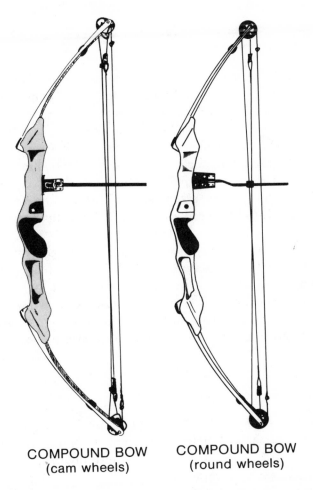

COMPOUND BOW
(cam wheels)

COMPOUND BOW
(round wheels)

less comfortably at full draw. This made shooting more pleasurable, because of the lower holding weight at full draw which was easier on fingers and muscles. And since a hunter should always shoot the heaviest draw he/she can handle *properly*—which is less than the peak weight he/she can draw and shoot once or twice but probably with little or no control—to gain maximum penetration potential, flatter trajectory, etc., you can understand this style of bow's popularity.

Field archers like the compound bow because it generally enables them to shoot a lighter weight arrow (compared to the arrow shot from a recurve of equal draw weight) and thus have a flatter trajectory. This, plus the increased ease of holding a lighter weight at full draw, enables many archers to aim better and thus shoot better. Lighter arrows often can be shot because less energy is being imparted to the arrow as the string is released and peak energy is imparted to the arrow after it is in forward motion. Peak energy delivered to an arrow already in motion will cause that arrow to bend less (in effect it acts like a stiffer arrow than it is) as it is launched, so a lighter, less stiff arrow can be shot. The trade-off is that lighter arrows are trickier to shoot and make tuning the bow/arrow combination more difficult. Heavier arrows are more forgiving, more stable. Recurve bows impart maximum energy to the arrow at the instant of release of the bowstring, and thus they need a stiffer arrow to withstand the impact properly.

The bows we shoot today are all quite efficient, generally converting 75%–85% of the energy stored in the bow into actual energy in the arrow. But they are not the most critical part of an archer's equipment; the arrows are—simply because good arrows, properly matched to a good quality bow, will give much better accuracy than mismatched arrows shot from the finest bow ever made.

ARROWS

"Straight as an arrow" is not fully appropriate, because an arrow—in the first few moments after release—is not straight at all. It actually bends as the force of the string pushes it into flight, creating what is known as the "archer's paradox."

This bending can be helpful, for it aids the arrow in clearing the bow. However, for better arrow performance, the bending should be held to the proper amount (for there can be too little, as well as too much, bending). This is why arrows must be matched to your bow.

You will note, on bows that are not center-shot, that the tip of the arrow points a fraction of an inch off center. So you would naturally expect the arrow to shoot off to the side somewhere instead of into the middle of the target. It would, if the string were pushing it in that direction—but the string is actually thrusting the arrow straight ahead, or nearly so.

As you release the bowstring, it rolls off your fingertips to the left (if you're a right-handed archer) of the direct line of thrust. Since the laws of physics decree that there must be an equal reaction for every action, the string—in its attempt to thrust straight forward—swings

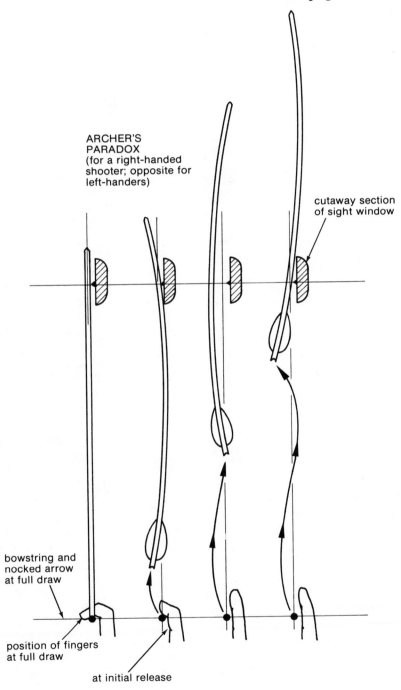

ARCHER'S
PARADOX
(for a right-handed
shooter; opposite for
left-handers)

cutaway section
of sight window

bowstring and
nocked arrow
at full draw

position of fingers
at full draw

at initial release

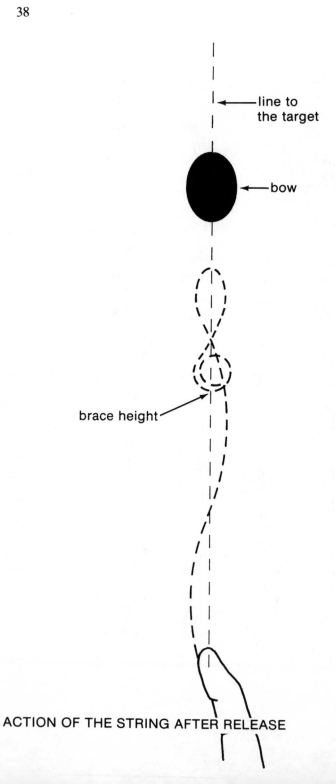

ACTION OF THE STRING AFTER RELEASE

back across the line of thrust and slightly to the right, then slightly to the left, of midline as it reaches brace height. Then it rotates back to static brace height in a sort of "S" movement. The string actually moves closer to the face of the bow than brace height before stopping completely at brace height.

Naturally, the nock of the arrow—which receives this sudden shock of energy upon release—must move with the bowstring to the left of center. As forward limb pressure, through the bowstring, tries to pull everything back into true center, the arrow tip is pushed right (for a right-handed archer) into the arrow shelf, which resists this pressure.

The major part of the arrow shaft is free to bend between these two pressure exertions. So it does. The degree of bend is controlled by the spine strength. A heavier spine will bend less, but will recover more slowly. An arrow will not strighten into true flight until about 20 yards, but it will have basically dampened the bending within 10 yards. For right-handed archers, an arrow spine too heavy will strike the target with the nock end to the right of center; spined too light, it will strike with the nock left of center. (For left-handed archers, the opposite occurs.

But before it reaches this point, the arrow goes through about 2¼-2½ bends (one right, one left, and beginning a second bend right) to clear the bow, and then several dampened bends as it flies. One left plus one right bend is called a spine "cycle."

The fractional beginning of the second right bend helps move the fletching away from the arrow rest, thus clearing the bow smoothly.

Actually, a properly shot arrow should touch the arrow rest for as short a distance as possible after the shot. The rest thus cannot exert a drag on the arrow, and the arrow is freer to recover properly with better speed.

The string continues to accelerate the arrow until well past the mid-range of limb recovery, but since the arrow is in motion the bending of the arrow will be less (there's less resistance from a moving object than from a stationary object). The controlling effects of the fletching, arrow spine, and air friction will continue the damping of the arrow's bending.

The center-shot bow is designed to minimize these deflections by allowing the arrow to be positioned as nearly as possible in the same direction of thrust as the bowstring.

Fletching helps stabilize the arrow into smooth flight. However, fletching can give too much control or too little control. A longer and lower fletch style will give better control than a short, high fletch, even though they have the same area. On the short, high fletch, the rear barbs would lie down considerably in flight and thus be of no value. The longer, lower fletch will also clear the bow more easily.

Feathers must be affixed to the shaft so the wind pressure strikes the underside of the feather. This side is smooth, will create better air flow, and will support the pressure.

Plastic vanes don't have the problems of feathers. They are smooth on both sides, which reduces surface friction, and they will not lie down. So a smaller vane than a feather can be used, with equal results. In fact, the smaller vane will be lighter, so the arrow will have increased cast.

However, since vanes will not lie down, bow clearane can—and often does—become more of a problem. More skillful bow tuning is needed with vanes.

The arrow must spin in flight, if it is to be stabilized quickly. Some spin is imparted from the string, so even a straight fletch will give stabilization. The spiral and helical fletches will impart even more stabilizing effect; but the final choice is a matter of personal preference. A higher degree of offset will stabilize an arrow more quickly, but it will also slow the arrow more quickly, simply because of increased drag.

GLOSSARY

Archery has a language peculiarly its own. Know that language, and great doors of understanding will swing open. Archery terms are your building blocks; you must have at least a rudimentary understanding of them to learn more, to ask intelligent questions, to know what your instructor is saying.

Look through the glossary carefully, It starts on page 181. You don't need to memorize everything right away; but you must become basically familiar with the fundamental terms.

chapter two

getting ready to shoot

ARE YOU RIGHT-EYED OR LEFT-EYED?

All people know whether they are right-handed or left-handed. But ask a person which of his eyes is dominant, and the reply may be a blank stare. Few people, unless they are archers or opticians, realize that they have a dominant eye, and that one's "good" eye isn't always one's dominant eye.

To shoot a bow to your best potential, you should shoot on the side of your dominant eye. That is because the dominant eye automatically aligns any object projected in front of it. The nondominant eye adds the dimension of vision to permit accurate depth perception.

FINDING YOUR DOMINANT EYE

To find your dominant eye, extend both arms in front of you with open palms toward the target. Make a triangular opening by overlapping thumbs and fingers.

41

Make a triangle with your thumbs and open hands. Extend the triangle to arm's length toward the target center.

With both eyes open, look through this triangular opening at the bull's-eye. Be sure you keep the triangular opening small so you cannot see through it with both eyes. Now, keeping both eyes open, slowly bring the hand triangle back toward your face, keeping the bull's-eye in the triangle.

The hand triangle will end up in front of your dominant eye.

As a double check of eye dominance, extend your arms again and, *without moving hands or head,* close your left eye. If the bull's-eye remains in the opening, your right eye is dominant and you should shoot right-handed. If, when you close your left eye, you find yourself staring at the back of your right hand, then your left eye is dominant and you should shoot left-handed.

You will see this view through the hand triangle.

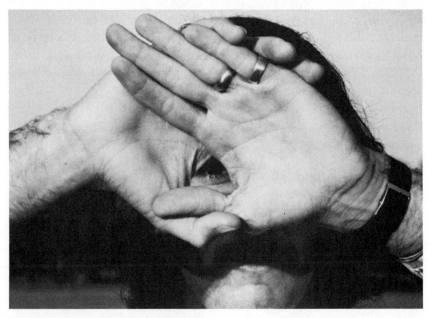

Now bring your hands back to your face, without increasing the size of the triangle. You will automatically bring the triangle to the front of your dominant eye.

It is highly recommended that you shoot on the dominant eye side. Doing so will give you five advantages: (1) you can shoot with both eyes open; (2) this allows more light on the target; (3) there will be less eye and facial fatigue (squinting or closing one eye shot after shot is tough work); (4) also better depth perception; (5) also natural vision alignment.

If you shoot with your nondominant eye, you'll probably have double vision, you will shoot radically to the side, and you will have blurred targets and continual alignment problems.

This is one situation in life where asserted dominance is welcome. (There are some people, but not many, who do not have a dominant eye; they can shoot from whichever side they choose.)

BRACING THE BOW

Once you've made the dominant eye test, and have chosen the appropriate right- or left-handed archery equipment, you're ready to start shooting.

Almost.

And that's because you've got to brace or string the bow, brace it right, and know why you should brace it right. The reasons are economical and healthful. Improper bracing can: (1) ruin a beautiful bow by breaking or twisting a limb; (2) punch out your eye and/or do other facial damage. Either way, you lose. Usually, so does the bow.

There are three basic ways to string a bow: the step-through method, the push-pull method, and with a bow stringer (the best way, by far).

Bow Stringer

This is a single string, several inches longer than the bowstring itself, with leather or plastic cups at each end. Usually one cup is larger than the other. Place the smaller cup on the tip of the upper limb, because the bowstring must slide slightly up under it to fit into the string groove on the limb tip.

Hold your bow horizontally in your strongest hand and place the bow stringer under the arch of either foot. Check to be sure the string is

BRACING THE BOW WITH A BOW STRINGER. Slip the leather cups over the limb tips (larger cup on the lower limb tip), place your foot in the middle of the bow stringer, and pull up. As you pull with one hand, slide the bowstring toward the upper limb tip and slip it into the notches. Be sure the bow stringer is considerably longer than your bowstring, or you will gain no leverage. Also be sure the bow stringer has not slipped off the side of the recurve of either limb when you begin to apply lift pressure.

securely placed in the grooves on the lower limb tip. Place thumb and index finger against the string loop on the upper limb and slide the loop up the limb as you smoothly and steadily pull up on the bow with your strong hand. When the loop slips into the string grooves, you can slide your index or other fingers under the limb to double check it as you slowly release the tension on the bow stringer.

Be sure you have a bow stringer with large enough caps to fit properly on the limb tips, and be sure you draw the bow perfectly vertical above the bow stringer. A string with too small caps will keep slipping off the tips, and if you don't draw the bow in a perfect line, the bow stringer will also slip off.

Be sure you have even pressure on both limbs as you pull the bow up; unless it's an extremely light bow, you won't be able to string it if it's unbalanced.

Don't use a string so long that it doesn't tighten up until you have lifted the bow to your waist. On the other hand, don't use a bow stringer that's just barely longer than the bow; these shorter bow stringers create an improperly sharp angle from the bow tip to your foot and are tough to use without having the bow twist sideways. A bow stringer that becomes tight when you have the bow somewhere between your knee and hip will give the best angles and leverage, allowing you to use your back muscles to full advantage.

This method, because it allows uniform tension on bow limbs and creates less danger to you, is the best way to string a bow. However, since it involves another piece of equipment—the bow stringer—and is slower than the other methods, it is not as widely used as it should be, especially among bowhunters.

Push-Pull

Place the lower limb tip against an instep, with the hand of the same side (right instep, right hand) grasping the bow handle (the actual hand area, not the sight window), and the index finger and thumb of the other hand against the string loop on the upper limb. It would probably help keep the bow string in the groove and limb notches on the lower limb if you were to push against the upper limb loop before you begin the push-pull method by placing the lower limb tip against an instep.

Place your feet far enough apart to give you leverage *and* balance. As you begin to PULL upward against the handle of the bow, PUSH downward and away from you with the extended arm on the upper limb. Keep your face behind the shoulder of your extended arm by

PUSH-PULL METHOD. Brace the lower limb tip against your foot. Then pull toward you with the hand on the handle riser, pushing down and away with the hand on the upper limb, sliding the string toward the notches as you push. The danger in this method is that if your pushing hand slips, the bow could fly forward and hit your face. Also, if you have a very long and/or heavy draw weight bow, you will find it difficult to use this method.

48

pulling your head down, or roll your shoulder into the line between your head and the bow as you push-pull. This will give you as much facial protection as possible with this bracing method.

Continue to push-pull until the upper bowstring loop slides into the side notches on the limb and into the small groove in the middle of the recurve. Then after you have straightened up, visually check *both* limb tips to be sure the string is set properly.

This method is the easiest and fastest, and most people use it, despite the potential danger.

Step-Through

This method gives you the most leverage on the bow; it also offers the most opportunity to inadvertently twist a limb or limbs. Used carefully, it is acceptable; and because of the leverage many weaker archers use it.

Place one leg between the bow and the string. Hook the lower limb tip firmly around the front of your other ankle, so the belly of the bow is behind you. Check the lower nock to be sure the string is properly seated. Assume a comfortable upright stance, with feet far enough apart to give you good balance, and have the back of the thigh fitted against the lower part of the handle riser.

Raise the heel of the foot at the bow tip slightly, to help prevent twisting of the bow limbs. Bend the upper limb forward with the power hand (right hand if bow is behind right thigh), being careful to pull forward in a straight line with the limb's natural movement. Pull over your thigh and hip, not toward your body. Pulling toward your body will twist the limb.

Simply slide the string loop upward as you pull and check its seating in the grooves as you smoothly release the muscle tension.

The braced bow now possesses stored energy; when drawn, it will possess much more stored energy—a potentially dangerous amount of stored energy if the string is not seated properly in the notches and grooves at both limb tips.

So after you've braced, or strung, a bow by any method, pick it up,

STEP-THROUGH METHOD. Place the lower limb in front of one foot and step between the riser and bowstring with the other foot. Pull the upper limb forward over your thigh and slide the string into the limb tip notches. The weakness of this method is that you often tend to pull the upper limb toward your body instead of in a straight line with the bowstring and the natural bending of the bow. The resulting uneven pressure can easily twist a limb.

look at both tips, then sight down the tense bowstring to be sure that both limbs are in perfect alignment. If one is twisted, you should be able to determine it with this test.

Put on your shooting accessories, because NOW you're ready to shoot!

chapter three

basic shooting technique

A good archer is a model of controlled strength and consistency. His/her moves are smooth, graceful. The better the archer, the less he appears to work and the more beautiful this becomes, as he places shot after shot in the center of the target.

Yet, the champion is doing almost exactly the same thing you will do when you shoot your first arrow. The steps of an archery shot are precise and must be followed in order. They are basically simple; only as your skills and knowledge of the intricacies of archery increase will you begin to notice the differences in shooting style and technique possessed by top-flight archers.

When you begin, seek out good coaching or carefully follow an instruction book—this one, I hope. If you're going to learn to shoot, you're ahead of the game if you learn it the right way. Too many archers who imagine themselves direct descendants of Robin Hood and second cousin to Hiawatha regard instruction as needless waste of time. Then they proceed to teach themselves half a dozen bad faults, blame their archery tackle, and practically tie themselves into pretzels. Then, and only then, when all seems lost, they ask for help. And since shooting a bow requires grooving several physical and mental actions into an almost unconscious act, they and their new-found coach are confounded with hangups before they even step to the shooting line to learn the correct way.

Start right, and you'll reach surprising plateaus of success. One lesson should have you hitting a reasonably large, close target consistently. Succeeding plateaus will be reached more slowly—you have to pay your dues in every sport.

Once you learn the basics, you will begin to develop as a thinking archer, developing the best possible personal form. The most important element to remember—in basic and in more skilled shooting—is that you must master one step or technique before you can advance to the next. Work from a *positive* attitude, building on your strengths, on the things you do right.

It's human nature to tell yourself, "I'm doing this wrong and that wrong, and three or four other things, too." Resist that temptation. Tell yourself, "Here's what I'm doing right. Now I'll build the rest of my shot sequence on these good points. And when I get one more part of my shot developed into a consistent strength, I'll work on the next problem."

This is a *positive* attitude. It's valuable. Develop it right along with your shooting strengths.

THE BASIC ARCHERY SHOT

Now let's begin at the beginning. You have a bow properly fitted to your strength. You've drawn it a couple of times and can hold it steadily at full draw without shaking. You have arrows matched to your bow's draw weight at your draw length. Your finger tab and armguard are in place. Chest protector, too, if you wish.

Stance

Take an open stance, straddling the shooting line. Your back foot will be parallel to the shooting line, and your forward foot will be at about a 45-degree angle between the shooting line and the target. Your feet will be about shoulder-width apart, with weight distributed evenly onto both feet.

This stance gives excellent balance and prevents natural body sway. You have stability in the wind. You have a wider range of movement from your hips and waist—for target and hunting shots. (You must make a conscious effort to place your feet in the same place for every shot. If possible, mark your foot positions with a felt-tip pen or something similar. This is the first step in developing consistency of form.)

BASIC ARCHERY SHOT SEQUENCE: STANCE

Nock an Arrow

Make the sequence as simple as possible, with minimum movement. Use the exact sequence each time.

Use a double nocking point, one above and one below the position on the string where the arrow will be nocked. This adds confidence to your nocking movements and string placement, and ensures that your arrow will be on the string in the same place every time. A single nock will allow the arrow to slide down the string sometimes, especially when you haven't yet developed the habit of keeping it firmly nocked in position.

Be sure the nock fits the bowstring snugly. This prevents the arrow from falling off the string as you draw the bow and keeps you from releasing the string when the arrow isn't fully nocked.

The odd, or cock, feather must point away from the string at right angles. The two hen feathers will lie next to the string.

NOCKING AN ARROW

String Hand

Form a Boy Scout salute with the first three fingers of your bow hand. This positions your hand to receive the string, keeps your little finger off the string, folds your thumb against your palm, and positions it at an angle that will fit under your cheekbone or jawbone at anchor.

Place the string deep in the first crease of your finger joints, or just back of the first joint. Your fingers will curl around the string, forming a deep hook. This will give you a confident hold on the string and will keep the arrow from falling off the arrow rest or shelf.

STRING HAND

Keep the back of your hand straight with your arm and relax your wrist. The tension should be only in your fingers.

Bow Hand and Bow Arm

Your bow should fit in the V of index finger and thumb, with the finger and thumb forming a loose ring around the bow handle. The bow will be held against the muscle pad below your thumb. With a loose finger/thumb ring, your hand will conform to the shape of the bow handle and will prevent flinching when you release.

Your fingers and wrist on the bowstring will be relaxed.

Now turn the bottom of your bow arm elbow away from the string and hold your elbow stiff. Lock it if you can. Turning your elbow away from the string will give better string clearance, keeping the string from stinging your bow arm on release. Use a long armguard as protection; your shooting form isn't grooved yet and the long guard will cover for the errant releases.

BOW HAND AND BOW ARM

Head Up/Shoulders Back

Now raise your head to vertical and look at the center of the target. Your bow hand, elbow, and string hand are still in the position set earlier. This now becomes the unit. You're in a basic transition step that establishes a *positive* target attitude and unit position. While you're in this position, you can recheck your bow hand, bow arm, and string finger position.

HEAD UP AND SHOULDERS BACK

Raise the Unit; Predraw Aim

Raise your bow arm and draw arm to shoulder height. If you are aiming without a bowsight (called "instinctive" aiming) with both eyes open, position the tip of the arrow about 18 inches below the target center (using a 36-inch target face, standing 20-30 feet from the target). Shift your eyes to the center of the target and concentrate on the very center of the target without moving the unit. This is "gap" aiming.

If you are aiming with a bowsight, place the sight in the middle of the target and maintain this general sight location.

RAISE THE UNIT; PREDRAW AIM

RAISE THE UNIT; PREDRAW AIM

The predraw "gap" aiming method lets you aim prior to the stress of full draw. It puts your bow arm in the proper position with the target, gives a consistent basic aiming technique, and you won't be preoccupied with aiming at full draw. You can concentrate on your form. However, this is effective only at close range—up to twenty yards. But when you're beginning, you should not be any farther than that from the target; closer would be better.

The bowsight method gives you a simple, positive aiming procedure. You have constant visual reference on your sight placement. However, with a bowsight, you can overemphasize the sighting procedure and lose concentration on your form. And at this stage of development, you should be concentrating primarily on form.

With either sighting technique you must emphasize arrow grouping rather than bull's-eye hits. Bull's-eye hits will happen, but the grouping of arrows tells whether or not you're performing the shot sequence identically each time, and also tells you how well you're performing it.

Concurrent to form development, it is extremely important that you concentrate on the spot you intend to hit with the arrow. This will help develop the concentration needed, and will guide your efforts into a smooth repetition of action leading to a properly executed shot.

Full Draw with Side Anchor or Under-the-Chin Anchor

Maintain the predraw aim or sight position and keep your bow arm straight, elbow locked. Draw the string by pulling with your shoulder *and* back muscles. It should feel like your shoulder blades are pulling toward each other. Your drawing elbow should be slightly higher than the drawing shoulder. To anchor, touch the corner of your mouth with your index finger while your thumb slides along and drops behind and under your jaw.

Using the under-the-chin anchor, you must draw slightly closer to the bow arm because you're coming in closer under the chin. Your draw will also be slightly lower than for the side anchor, possibly almost toward your collarbone. Draw back low enough that the string contacts the nose and chin first. After the contact is made between nose and chin, with your drawing hand about 1½ inches below the base of your chin, slide your string hand and forearm and elbow up as a unit. As you do

FULL DRAW WITH SIDE ANCHOR

FULL DRAW WITH UNDER-THE-CHIN ANCHOR

this, the string will slide upward, keeping contact with chin and nose. Move the drawing unit upward until the string fingers and hand contact the chin and edge of the jawbone. This method makes it easier to attain a firm, positive position under the chin, as opposed to drawing straight back under it or coming in and under from the side of the face. Your drawing elbow might be slightly lower with this anchor than in the side anchor, but only because the entire drawing unit is lower.

Maintain full draw by constant pulling from shoulder and back muscles. The high drawing elbow gives you better alignment and tension. Your anchor must feel secure at all times; it will feel this way if you locate it at a position that's simple to duplicate on each shot. Your anchor, then, becomes the rear sight.

Hold and Aim

You have pre-aimed your bow, so concentrate on the very center of the target and hold the sight position there. At the same time, you will have a constant feeling of tension in drawing arm, shoulder, and back muscles. Since the target is stationary, but the sight is not, you must bring the sight to the target as you aim. Focus your eye on the target. Let the sight become blurred. Line the string on the iris of your eye and look "around" the string's fuzziness (it, too, will be out of focus) on both sides of the string. This takes care of string alignment and aiming. Now your eyes will concentrate on the center of the target while your mind concentrates on continuing the tension in your back muscles. Hold firmly and confidently for a slow count of three.

Release

With your eyes concentrating on the center of the target, and your anchor firm along your jaw, start pulling your shoulder blades together and your drawing elbow back. As this occurs, relax your string fingers. The increase in shoulder and back tension activates the string hand to relax. The release is activated by relaxing the entire string hand from your wrist forward, and the string feels like it's sliding in a smooth, straight line through your fingers.

UNDER-THE-CHIN FOLLOW-THROUGH

Follow-Through

As your string fingers slide along your jaw, touching the side of your neck, your bow remains in line with the target and your eyes continue concentrating on the center of the target. Hold this follow-through until you hear the arrow hit the target. Proper eye concentration on the center of the target will prevent flinching and peeking—your shooting

SIDE ANCHOR FOLLOW THROUGH

form should not fall apart when you release and follow through, but should remain positive and constant. And you should not see the arrow in flight; your bow hand and the bow itself will obscure it if you maintain proper form.

The follow-through should be a natural reaction of the increased back and shoulder tension which created the release; it should not be inhibited or forced.

These elements of the basic archery shot must all become part of a mental checklist. You will use this checklist every time you shoot an arrow. You will check certain parts of it as you prepare to draw, as you are at full draw, as you follow through, and as you mentally correct your form before beginning the next shot sequence.

By carefully following this checklist you will strengthen your form and increase your confidence. You will also check the tendency to shoot too fast. Fast shooting nearly always means you have not fully, carefully, and confidently prepared your form for each shot and have not aimed properly.

chapter four

enjoying archery: competition, games, bowhunting

Where can you enjoy archery?

The answer is: just about anywhere.

It has already been stated that you can shoot archery all by yourself, or with family or friends. You can shoot in schools and in your backyard. You can shoot in competitive archery under organized rules with definite reward goals, or you can make up your own games.

Since we are all relatively gregarious, the sport is generally more fun when we're with other like-minded people. You can find these people in any of the archery organizations given here, and you can find them in local clubs—a target club, field archery club, bowhunting club, sportsmen's club, or combinations of these. You might also check with the state Fish and Game Department, Information and Education section.

If you are searching for a local club, ask at a sport shop, a recreation department, or the local newspaper—or look in the telephone book's yellow pages. One of these sources should be able to tell you how to contact the local group.

Many clubs are affiliated with a national archery organization and the representative state organization. Look them over. Try all phases of archery. Subscribe to one of the archery publications listed below. Find the club that most nearly matches your archery interests. Then join the club and have fun.

You can shoot in your back yard with friends.

You can shoot in organized competition.

NATIONAL ORGANIZATIONS

National Archery Association of the U.S.A. (NAA), 1750 E. Boulder St., Colorado Springs, CO 80909, is the official amateur archery organization in the United States. It is a member of the *Féderation Internationale de Tir à l'Arc (FITA)* and of the U.S. Olympic Committee. The NAA's stated purpose is ". . . to perpetuate, foster and direct the practice of archery in the United States in accordance with the high spirit and honorable tradition of that most ancient sport." Its efforts paid big dividends in 1972 at Munich, West Germany, when archery made its initial appearance as a recognized Olympic sport. The United States returned with two gold medals from that archery competition, with John Williams winning the men's division and Doreen Wilber winning the women's division.

The NAA conducts a varied program, including national indoor and outdoor target championships; a national field championship; indoor winter league tournament; adult, intercollegiate, and high school mail matches; a national flight tournament; team tryouts for target and field Championships of the Americas, International and Olympic competition; a Junior Olympic Archery Development (JOAD) program; certified instructor programs throughout the country; sanctioning of the intercollegiate national championships; plus the sanctioning of regional, state, and local NAA-affiliated tournaments. NAA-certified instructors travel internationally to coach the teams of other nations and help develop their archery programs. The National Crossbowmen of the U.S.A. are also affiliated with the NAA and compete at the same tournaments in their own division.

World target championships are held every odd-numbered year and world field championships are held every even-numbered year. Tryouts are held one to two months before each event.

Since everyone enjoys competition more when competing on his own skill level, the NAA has a classification system and age brackets. The American Round (30 arrows at 60 yards, 30 arrows at 50 yards, and 30 arrows at 40 yards) is the classification round. The classes are AA, A, B, and C. To reach class AA, men must score 1400 or better and women 1300 or better; class A, men 1250 to 1399 and women

Doreen Wilber, women's 1972 Olympic archery champion (shown here shooting at the NAA National Championships).

1150 to 1299; class B, men 1000 to 1249 and women 950 to 1149; class C, men below 1000 and women below 950.

The age brackets are: senior men and women, 18 years or over; intermediate boys and girls, 15 to 18 years; junior boys and girls, 12 to 15 years; cadet boys and girls, under 12. Archers may shoot in a higher bracket than their own if they wish, but not in a lower bracket.

Championship rounds in NAA competition include the American, 900, and men's and women's FITA. Number of arrows and distances for the American Round have already been given. The 900 Round has

The first U.S. Olympic archery team (1972) Back row, from left:
Ed Eliason, Linda Myers, John Williams, Doreen Wilber,
Maureen Bechdolt, Dennis McComak. Lower left, George
Helwig, team manager; lower right, C.R. Fowkes, team coach.

John Williams shooting in the
1974 NAA National Target
Championships, pro division.

Scoring at the #1 women's amateur target at the 1974 NAA National Target Championships.

30 arrows at 60 yards, 30 at 50 yards, and 30 at 40 yards, just as in the American Round. However, the 900 Round is shot at a 10-ring scoring system on the 48-inch face.

The men's and women's FITA Round have 10-ring scoring also. Men shoot 36 arrows at 90 meters (122-centimeter face), 36 arrows at 70 meters (122-centimeter face), 36 arrows at 50 meters (80-centimeter face), and 36 arrows at 30 meters (80-centimeter face). Women shoot the same number of arrows, but they shoot at 70, 60, 50, and 30 meters. They also shoot at a 122-centimeter face on the two longer distances and an 80-centimeter face on the two shorter distances. Perfect score for the FITA Round is 1440.

Here are some nonchampionship and historical rounds:

The Columbia Round	48''	*The Hereford Round*	48''
24 arrows at 50 yards		72 arrows at 80 yards	
24 arrows at 40 yards		48 arrows at 60 yards	
24 arrows at 30 yards		24 arrows at 50 yards	
The Junior American Round	48''	*The Junior Columbia Round*	48''
30 arrows at 50 yards		24 arrows at 40 yards	
30 arrows at 40 yards		24 arrows at 30 yards	
30 arrows at 30 yards		24 arrows at 20 yards	
The St. George Round	48''	*The National Round*	48''
36 arrows at 100 yards		48 arrows at 60 yards	
36 arrows at 80 yards		24 arrows at 50 yards	
36 arrows at 60 yards			
The Team Rounds	48''	*The York Round*	48''
96 arrows at 60 yards (Men)		72 arrows at 100 yards	
96 arrows at 50 yards (Women)		48 arrows at 80 yards	
		24 arrows at 60 yards	
The Duryee Round	80cm.	*The Chicago Round*	16''
(ten ring scoring)		96 arrows at 20 yards	
90 arrows at 30 yards			
The "300" Indoor Round	16''	*The Easton Round*	48''
(5 arrows an end,		(scored 5-4-3-2-1)	
scored 5-4-3-2-1)		20 arrows at 60 yards	
black and white face		20 arrows at 50 yards	
60 arrows at 20 yards		20 arrows at 40 yards	

For indoor competition, the Chicago, 300, Duryee, and PAA Indoor Rounds are most often shot.

Two international indoor rounds have also been adopted and are being increasingly used. They are the FITA Short Round, shot at 18 meters (19 yards, 1 foot, 9 inches) on a 40-centimeter (15.7-inch) face, and the FITA Long Round, shot at 25 meters (27 yards, 1 foot, .029 inches) on a 60-centimeter (23.6-inch) face. Both targets are 10-ringed in proportion to FITA faces, with FITA colors, and score 10-9-8-7-6-5-4-3-2-1. A round is 30 arrows in 10 ends of three arrows each.

National Field Archery Association of the U.S.A. (NFAA), Route 2, Box 514, Redlands, California 92373, is a participant's organization for field archers that encourages use of the bow in the hunting of all legal game, the furtherance and protection of the sport of bowhunting, and the conducting of public educational programs for field archery and bowhunting.

The NFAA sponsors state, regional, and national competition in field archery for amateurs and professionals. The field, hunter, and animal rounds are the basic rounds shot, although other rounds are also used.

The field round consists of the following 14 units: 15, 20, 25, and 30 yards at a 35 cm face (four arrows at each distance); 40, 45, and 50 yards at a 50 cm face (four arrows at each distance); 55, 60, and 65 yards at a 65 cm face (four arrows at each distance); plus the following four position shots, with each arrow to be shot from a different position or at a different target; 35 yards at a 50 cm target, all from the same distance, but from different positions or different targets; 30, 35, 40, and 45 yards at a 50 cm face; 50, 60, 70, and 80 yards at a 65 cm face and 20, 25, 30, and 35 feet at a 20 cm face. Scoring is five points for a bull's-eye, four points for the second scoring ring, and three points for the outer circle. A round consists of two complete 14 target units. Perfect score is 560.

The hunter round uses the same 14-target unit shot twice for a complete round and scored the same as the field round. Four target sizes (65 cm, 50 cm, 35 cm, and 20 cm) are used and there is a greater variety in shooting distances.

The animal round also uses 14-target units, with twice around for a complete score. Printed animal targets are used, with the scoring areas divided into two parts. Four scoring groups are used, with a different-sized scoring unit for each group. The first group has three targets with three walk-up shooting positions of a maximum distance of 60 yards and minimum of 40 yards. The second group has three targets with three walk-up positions of a maximum distance of 45 yards and minimum of 30. The third group has four targets with four one-position shots, 35-yard maximum distance and 20-yard minimum. The fourth group has four targets with four one-position shots, maximum distance of 20 and minimum of 10 yards.

Three-dimensional targets add interest to a field shoot.

A maximum of three arrows may be shot at each target, with only the highest scoring arrow counting. Scoring is 20 or 16 for the first arrow, 14 or 10 for the second arrow, and 8 or 4 for the third arrow. Perfect score is 560 (28 targets, 20 points per arrow).

The NFAA also has amateur and professional shooting in indoor competition.

Shooters at a PAA National Championship event.

Professional Archers Association, (PAA), Box 24407, Mayfield Heights, OH 44124, promotes professionalism in archery; develops, sponsors, and promotes money tournaments; and operates its tournaments under a strict set of equipment and shooting rules. It also supports amateur archery and intercollegiate competition.

The PAA holds a national outdoor championship event and

Final-round competition at a recent PAA National Championship tournament.

sanctioned winter (indoor) and summer (outdoor) circuit of tournaments.

The outdoor PAA Round consists of a series of 10 black and white targets, shot twice. The targets are in five-yard increments from 20 through 65 yards. The first three distances are shot on a 14-inch face, the middle four on a 22-inch face and the final three on a 30-inch face.

Scoring is 5-4-3, with three arrows per end. A perfect score is 300.

The PAA Indoor Round, shot on a 16-inch blue and white face, consists of 60 arrows at 20 yards, with five arrows per end, shot in games of four ends. Scoring is 5-4-3-2; perfect score for one game is 100 and for a complete round is 300. The bull's-eye is 3.2 inches in diameter.

Archery Range and Retailers Organization (ARRO), 7626 W. Donges Bay, Mequon, WI 53092, has members throughout the country. These commercial archery ranges, which nearly always include a pro shop, retail sales, and archery instruction, operate winter and summer leagues. Leagues are organized for target and bowhunting archers. Many sponsor local tournaments.

Archery Manufacturers Organization (AMO), 200 Castlewood Rd., N. Palm Beach, FL 33408, is an organization of archery manufacturers working to develop all aspects of the sport of archery throughout the country through projects in archery education, standardization of equipment, publishing of archery instructional materials, and cooperation with state and federal lawmaking bodies in regard to hunting regulations.

Pope & Young Club, 6471 Richard Ave., Placerville, CA 95667, is the national record-keeping body for trophy big game taken by bowhunters in North America. It sponsors triennial competition and holds an awards banquet at the conclusion of each competition span.

American Archery Council (AAC), 200 Castlewood Rd., N. Palm Beach, 33408, is comprised of representatives from each of the national archery organizations. Its purpose is the support and promotion of all forms of archery.

ARCHERY PUBLICATIONS

Archery World, P.O. Box 27161, Minneapolis, MN 55427. Bimonthly.

Bow & Arrow, Box HH, Capistrano Beach, CA 92624. The official publication of the National Field Archery Association. Bimonthly.

Bowhunter, 3808 S. Calhoun St., Fort Wayne, IN 46807. Seven issues per year.

Pro Archer, 7315 N. San Anna Dr., Tucson, AZ 85704.
The official publication of the National Archery Association. Bimonthly.

ARCHERY GAMES

Tic-Tac-Toe

A target face is marked off in three rows of three squares each, just as in the regular tic-tac-toe game. Tie an inflated balloon in each square for increased visual and sound effects. Usual shooting distance is 15 yards. The first person or team to break three balloons in any line wins.

Wand Shooting

Place a strip of masking tape vertically on the target face from top to bottom. Shoot at 15 yards. Score a point when you hit the tape and set whatever total score for game you desire. You can shoot individually or in teams.

Bird Shooting

You will need flu-flu arrows, half a dozen circular cardboard discs (made by yourself or purchased), and a range that is safely clear for about 100 yards. One person throws the disc up, across, and about 10 yards in front of the shooters, who are standing with arrows nocked and bows ready. If you are more accurate shooters, move back five yards. Shoot as teams, or with one team member from each team shooting at a time. Most hits after a specified number of throws, or after a specified time, wins.

Bouncing Balloons

This works best on a breezy day. Use flu-flu arrows and shoot at balloons bouncing along the ground with the wind. Be sure the range beyond the balloons is safe because the arrows might skip. You may wish to use blunt arrow tips. This is excellent practice for rabbit hunting.

Bingo

Construct a simulated bingo card on a target face and shoot at an agreed-upon distance. First person or team to hit five squares in any line wins.

Swinging Ball

Suspend a soft rubber ball on a two-foot string from the top of a target. One person sets the ball in motion and then gets safely out of the way before the shooters are allowed to draw. Shoot at any agreed-upon distance. Score two points when the ball is pinned to the target and one point when it is hit but not pinned.

V Target

Cut a large V from an 18- or 24-inch target and fasten it to a mat. Mark scoring arcs within the V. The first archer shoots as low in the V as he can. His competitor must shoot as low or lower. Determine a game total score and point value of each scoring arc; first person to reach that total wins. You could add interest by ruling that each archer call his shot, subtracting the appropriate number of points if he hits outside the arc called, and adding only when he hits the arc called.

If shooters of unequal skill are competing, mark an inner V for the more skilled archer, who then is allowed to score only within the inner V.

Roving

Choose a field or forest away from personal and property hazards. Keep your shooting group reasonably small for most fun. The lead archer selects a target—clump of grass or dirt, stump, spot in a dirt bank, etc.—and shoots one arrow from whatever distance he chooses. Other archers then shoot one arrow. This rotation may be repeated at the same target, if you wish.

Whoever shoots closest to the called target chooses and shoots first at the next target, and the process is repeated.

This is excellent hunting practice because targets are at unmarked distances, of varying sizes, and can be shot at from unusual shooting positions or from behind chosen obstacles like tree branches or bushes, or uphill or downhill.

Archery Golf

This can be played on a regulation golf course, if the manager of the golf course permits, or you may want to construct your own course. There are several special archery golf courses throughout the country. Use one bow and three arrows—a flight arrow, an approach arrow, and a putting arrow (generally a flu-flu with a spike tip)—if you're serious. If you don't have the specialized arrows, just shoot and have fun with your regular arrows. The "cup" is a four-inch ball placed near the green cup. You must knock the ball from its post (if it is not lying on the ground) to hole out. Object, of course, is to use as few shots as possible over a nine- or 18-hole course. If you are shooting on a regulation golf course, you should be able to shoot under par. A skilled archery golf shooter can consistently beat a skilled golfer.

Clout Shooting

The target for this long-range game is a 48-foot diameter circle laid out on the ground in concentric scoring rings. Men and intermediate boys shoot 36 arrows at 180 yards; women and intermediate girls shoot 36 arrows from 140 yards and juniors and cadets shoot 36 arrows from 120 yards. A flag marks the center of the target. A color-coded chain is attached to the stake holding the flag and is swept in a circle to score the arrows.

Shooting in the Crossbow Clout competition at the 1974 NAA Target Championships.

Running Deer

Suspend a cardboard deer target from a rope that is looped through pulleys on two posts set 15 or 20 yards apart. A pulling rope, attached to the support rope, will let a nonshooter move the deer and be safely out of shooting range. The rope operator can add variety to the game by suddenly stopping and starting the deer target, or jerking it so it bounces much like a running deer.

If you do not have an adequate backstop for this system, insert cardboard circles in old tires and roll them down an uneven slope. The bouncing tires will simulate running deer.

Archers shooting at a motor-and-cable-driven running deer target.

BOWHUNTING

Bowhunting is one of the fastest growing segments of the sport of archery. There are now more than 1.7 million licensed bowhunters in the United States, and countless thousands more who bowhunt for small game and varmints under other licenses.

Pennsylvania and Michigan top the list of licensed bowhunters with more than 200,000 each. Other top bowhunting states are Wisconsin, New York, Texas, California, and New Jersey. Most of these licenses are bought for the expressed purpose of deer hunting, since the whitetail and mule deer species are the major two animals hunted with the bow, although elk, pronghorn, and black bear have become popular.

Bowhunting is a true challenge; that's why so many sportsmen are taking up the sport. To be successful with his limited-range weapon, the bowhunter must study the species he hunts and learn its habits, he

Hunting deer from tree stands is becoming an extremely popular method.

must be a relatively good woodsman, and he must also be a good archer.

There's no better time of year to be afield than during the late summer, autumn, and early winter. You see a wide range of weather conditions, you observe firsthand the changing seasons, and you see and learn about countless forms of wildlife while you're afield. In short, you get a complete education in the workings of nature.

Bowhunters appreciate all the elements of hunting. How else would you explain the growth of a sport that has only about a five-percent hunter-success ratio?

Bowhunting Equipment

Most recurve hunting bows range from 48 inches to 64 inches. This is considerably shorter than recurve target bow lengths. The shorter length gives you more maneuverability in brush and when shooting from blinds or tree stands.

However, the shorter the bow, the more problems with sharp string angle at full draw, causing finger pinch and making the release more difficult. This also causes sore fingers, especially to bowhunters with draw lengths longer than 28 inches. The shorter bows, since they are lighter in virtual mass weight, are less stable and more difficult to shoot than longer bows. You sacrifice stability for maneuverability.

Longer bows are easier to shoot because they are more stable and smoother in draw. Many people prefer to buy a recurve hunting bow in the 60-inch to 64-inch length. The sacrifice in maneuverability is generally not highly critical, unless you will be hunting in very dense brush, and the longer length is easier to practice with over longer periods of time. Because of its smoothness of draw and stability, you will enjoy shooting it more.

If you're going to be a one-bow hunter and prefer a recurve, a 60-inch to 64-inch bow is all-around best.

Most compound bows run 40 to 50 inches axle to axle. Shooting principles remain the same regarding weight and length, but since these bows do not have long limbs, their overall length cannot be judged the same as recurves regarding finger pinch. A 48-inch compound will not cause the finger pinch a 48-inch recurve will, but a 40-inch compound could be expected to feel similar to a 48-inch recurve.

Bow Draw Weight: The average hunting bow should be 40–45 pounds for beginners and women. Check your state hunting regulations; a few states do not allow bows this light.

In all cases it is best to start with a light bow until you learn shooting form. Then, as your strength builds, you can work up to heavier hunting weights. The key in bowhunting is to use the heaviest bow you can shoot accurately, because you will get flatter arrow trajectory and better results on game. Thus, you will be much better off with a 45-pound bow that you can bring to *full draw* and shoot accurately than you will with a 55-pound bow that you cannot bring

John Williams on a Texas javelina hunt.

to full draw. A 45-pound bow brought to full draw will give better arrow performance—and thus better arrow penetration in big game— than a heavier bow brought to less than full draw. Only at full draw is the full power potential of a bow developed.

The laminated wood-glass recurve is a good bow to start with. It produces a good combination of speed, lightness, beauty, and shooting characteristics. And you can buy a good first hunting bow without breaking your bank account.

The compound bow, which has been well accepted by bowhunters, generally has more stored energy at full draw, giving the bowhunter the opportunity to draw a good weight, yet hold a lesser weight quite comfortably. These bows are generally more expensive than recurves and for beginners will usually be more difficult to tune satisfactorily. An inexpensive compound can be a good choice for a beginning bowhunter; a wide variety of models are available.

Arrow Material: The economy of wood shafts is offset by short life, warping tendencies, and high variability in spine and grain weight. Fiberglass is more uniform, more durable, and more expensive than wood. Aluminum is obviously the most uniform, is long lasting because it can be straightened after impact with a rock or similar object, and has the advantage of being available in many spine ranges and grain weights. Aluminum arrows are also the most expensive— generally about $3 per arrow. You must weigh all the factors and choose whichever arrow shaft best meets your personal criteria.

Fletching: Bright colors or totally white fletching usually work best because they can be seen most easily by the shooter. This is important in spotting the hit. Once in a while you will spook game because of the brightness but the advantages of seeing the exact location of a hit in low light conditions—when most game is seen and most shots are taken—far outweigh the spooking potential.

Preferences are fairly evenly split between feather and plastic fletching. Plastic fletching is silent and impervious to water and works best under damp conditions, but feather fletching is more forgiving and lighter weight. Selection is a personal choice. Feathers can be waterproofed with dry-fly dope. For best arrow flight, fletches should be applied with a helical twist.

Accessories: You will need a leather glove or double-layered finger tab; a long, fairly thick armguard to keep the sleeve on your bow arm clear of the string path; a camouflage sock for the bow limbs, or camouflage tape, or flat, woodsy-color spray paint to cut bow glare; string silencers to cut the sound of the string on release (to prevent spooking of game while the arrow is in flight); cable silencers on compound bows; an arrow holder to keep arrow in place on arrow rest; solidly placed nocking point locator so you can confidently nock the arrow against it even when you aren't looking at the nock; a safe bow, belt, or back quiver with a hood to cover the broadheads; good camouflage clothing and camouflage grease or paste for the backs of your hands and for your face, or camouflage gloves and headnet. PLUS: a belt pack that can carry an extra bowstring, knife, sharpening stone or file, matches, rope, first aid kit, etc.

Camouflage is a boon to the bowhunter.

Broadheads: No matter what brand or style you use, the most important thing is that they must be extremely sharp. Only heads that employ actual razor blades are sharp enough to use from the package. All others must be honed properly before use. The reason they must be razor-sharp is a broadhead is effective primarily through cutting and hemorrhage; it does not have significant shock factor. And a sharper broadhead will produce better penetration.

Broadheads are primarily available in two-blade, three-blade, four-blade, and five-blade design. Six-blade heads are also available. Some

Sharp broadheads are a must for all bowhunting. This hunter prepares his broadheads for the next day's hunt.

four-blade heads have four solid edges; others have a basic two-blade design with a smaller two-blade insert that locks into a slot in the head. This insert must also be sharpened properly to be effective.

Broadheads must be mounted properly, or they will cause erratic arrow flight. Spin a mounted broadhead on a shaft; if it spins smoothly with no wobble, it is balanced. Mount broadheads with hot waterproof glue or epoxy so they will adhere after impact.

This is not the problem it once was, for most broadheads today are of the razorblade-insert style with a threaded ferrule that screws into an insert. These are machined to close tolerances and are less likely to be off-center but should be checked before being shot.

How to Begin

There's a lot of difference between a bowhunter and a person in the woods with a bow and some arrows. So seek a competent instructor or dealer. Shoot the bow before you buy it. See whether you can draw and hold it and shoot it accurately for several shots. Your proper bow weight will also depend on the game you are seeking; larger animals demand the use of a heavier bow, which means you will have to practice considerably to learn to handle it properly.

Buy properly matched equipment that will fit your shooting style, your size, and your strength. Be prepared to spend several hours each week—for a couple of months prior to your hunt—practicing useful shooting techniques and judging distances. By "useful shooting techniques," we mean practicing shooting from a half-crouch, twisting the body to right or left before the shot, canting the bow to practice shooting between tree limbs, shooting over or around bushes, shooting almost straight down out of tree stands, etc. You will seldom have an opportunity to assume the classical target stance when shooting at game. And in bowhunting the first shot must count. You rarely will get a second shot at big game.

The true challenge in bowhunting is in the sacrifice you are willing to provide in proper practice, knowing that you have accepted the handicap of a historical weapon that demands the ultimate of your skill. When you've done this—when you've paid the price—you will understand that the challenge of the chase has superseded the event of the success. This is the growing sport of bowhunting, and the good bowhunter is willing to give the time and effort to get his game cleanly and efficiently.

Bowhunting Styles

There are three main styles: standing, stalking, and driving.

The stand hunter finds a good location along a deer trail, near the edge of a field where the game feeds morning and evening, or near a waterhole. Then he positions himself, preferably downwind, and waits. He might choose to wait in a ground blind constructed of strategically placed brush, or stand beside a tree or bush that breaks his outline, or position himself 8 to 12 feet above ground in a tree. If in a tree, he either stands on a limb or on one of the commercially available tree stands.

Hunting from a tree stand.

The stalking bowhunter seeks areas where game either beds down or feeds. Then he very slowly and carefully walks this area. This style demands all the skill and patience a bowhunter can develop. As a result, a successful stalk can be one of the most exciting types of hunting.

In driving game, a few hunters position themselves on trails around a specific area while other hunters move in from the opposite side of the area and hope to move game onto the waiting hunters. This can be an effective method, but most shots are taken at running game, which obviously are not the most desirable shots. Also, great groups of hunters moving into an area often do not project the most desirable public image, looking more like an army than true sporting hunters.

This basic description of the styles of hunting must be brief here because whole books can be, and have been, written on the many elements of bowhunting techniques. It is considerably different in many ways from rifle hunting. But once you have learned the basics, you can learn the finer points through experience and extended reading on the appropriate topics.

Bowfishing

Every state allows—and encourages—the taking of rough fish. Some states also allow the taking of game fish with archery tackle.

Common quarry are carp, buffalo, suckers, redhorse, gar, skates, and stingrays. Some of the more adventurous bowfishermen also seek shark.

Most bowfishing activity is in shallow water during the spring spawning seasons, although knowledgeable bowfishermen take rough fish all year. Some northern bowmen take pride in their ability to find carp during the cold winter months, when the unseasonable weather adds an extra element to shooting.

Your basic hunting bow will be adequate for bowfishing. You might want to reserve an old hunting bow for this use, since it may get knocked around or splashed with water quite often.

Other bowfishing equipment includes a reel (drum or heavy duty spin fishing), at least 90 feet of heavy braided line, solid fiberglass arrows, and special barbed fish points. Several varieties of fish points, some with retractable barbs and some with screw-off heads, are commercially available. Barbed heads are needed so the fish will not pull free.

Shallow water is preferred for bowfishing.

Many bowfishermen pursue carp from canoes.

The reel is attached to your bow at the base of the handle riser. This position is safely out of the way of your arrow and permits smooth paying out of line from the reel with the shot. Attach the line to the reel for arrow retrieval on missed shots and to help subdue the fish on a hit.

The solid, heavy fiberglass arrow is needed to aid in water penetration. Few effective shots are taken in water depths of more than four feet, because water density will stop an arrow rather quickly and it is difficult to gauge light refraction accurately at greater depths. The arrow will generally have a slip-on rubber fletching; some shooters remove the fletching, believing that its stabilizing effects at such short ranges on such a heavy arrow are practically nil.

The line is usually looped through a hole just ahead of the nock, and then run down through another hole in the fish point and head of the shaft, where it is tied. This gives a double securing system, should the line at the point break or the knot come loose.

You must be particularly safety-conscious with the line. If you inadvertently loop it around your wrist or the reel as you draw you will get a nasty burn or cut, or snap the line as you shoot.

Many local archery and sportsmen's clubs throughout the country sponsor carp contests each spring, awarding trophies and merchandise to the winners.

chapter five

intermediate archery

The key to good shooting is consistency—the ability to set up one perfect shot and then be able to duplicate it time after time. A good shooter looks almost like a machine. That shooter knows which shooting form works best for him. He knows his own best timing, from shot to shot and within each shot. He knows his equipment and how it performs.

The basic shooting technique has already been discussed in an earlier chapter. Now let's consider the variations in form.

How *you* develop your best form is entirely up to you and your coach. Watch any shooting line and you will soon note several slight variations on the basic principles—variations in stance, bow wrist, bow shoulder, anchoring styles, and degree of follow-through. These archers have all done their homework; they have found the form that best suits their physical structure, strength, and personal preferences.

What should *you* consider in developing confident, consistent shooting form? Here are some things to keep in mind:

Shooting style depends a lot on physical build: things like your weight relative to your bone structure and general frame type; the length of your forearms (which affects draw length and basically tells you how much you can be in line); the total length of your arm; and your chest structure.

Choose the form that is most comfortable. As long as you don't vary too much from the basic T of body and arm position you can do almost anything. And as long as you do it the same each time, it is right, no matter how wrong it may seem to other people.

STANCES

Open Stance

Pro: The open stance is used by most archers. It creates a secure base that is easily duplicated and minimizes natural body sway. It is stable in the wind and reduces overdrawing. The open stance gives maximum string clearance. The wide spread between shoulder blades allows better use of back and shoulder muscles. It moves the bow arm and shoulder away from the string on release and minimizes backward leaning. You are also facing the target in the follow-through, which minimizes neck strain.
Con: It may feel awkward in beginning stages, and you must remember to rotate at the waist to bring your shoulders in line with the target.

Closed Stance

Pro: This stance prevents body sway, is very stable, feels natural to self-taught archers, and brings the drawing elbow directly behind the arrow.
Con: It decreases string clearance, and you may become fatigued because you must twist more toward the target. It may also create a tendency to lean back and overdraw.

Square Stance

Pro: This is a natural body position, easy to arrive at and maintain.
Con: Natural body sway may be more difficult to control, so it may be difficult to use in the wind. Heavy-chested shooters may have trouble with string clearance.

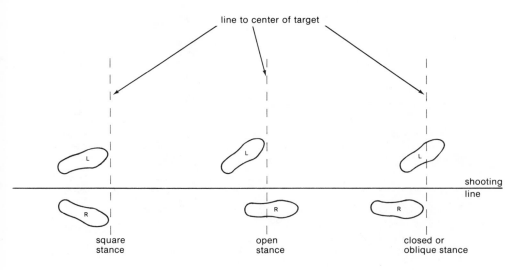

line to center of target

square
stance

open
stance

closed or
oblique stance

shooting
line

(These stances are for right-handed
shooter. Position of feet will be
reversed for left-handed shooter.)

BOW HAND

High Wrist

Pro: The high wrist provides a consistent location, because your hand easily finds a comfortable position on the throat of the bow handle. The small area of pressure minimizes bow torque and also aids bow performance. There is less of a tendency to grip the bow tightly or grab it on release.

Con: However, you may find this wrist position difficult to maintain properly under the constant tension in the wrist. A tense high wrist may move prior to release or during release, and it pulls the bow arm closer to the string path.

Low Wrist

Pro: The relaxed position of the bow hand reduces wrist fatigue, and

High wrist position

with pressure leading directly into the forearm from the base of the palm, there is less tendency for the wrist position to change over long shooting periods. The position is comfortable and easy to duplicate. The relaxed hand reduces torque potential on release and a sling will keep the hand in the proper position. Also, since hands are sympathetic, a relaxed bow hand helps relax the string hand.

Con: You may encounter a tension buildup and change in pressure point under tournament conditions, and you may develop a tendency to grab the bow upon release if the hand and wrist are not properly relaxed.

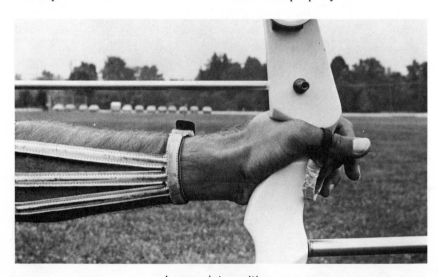

Low wrist position

Straight Wrist

Pro: This wrist is a very consistent grip, one in which you can usually tell whether you relax up or relax down; thus you can easily pinpoint an error if your wrist relaxes because the muscles in your forearm will tell you. There are not many muscles used with the straight wrist.
Con: If you have a weak wrist, this may not be a consistent wrist to use. No matter what your wrist strength, as you depress the web of skin between your thumb and palm, so much slack is taken out of the skin that the pressure tends to wrap the forefinger around the bow grip; if you do not properly control this you may grip the bow too tightly.

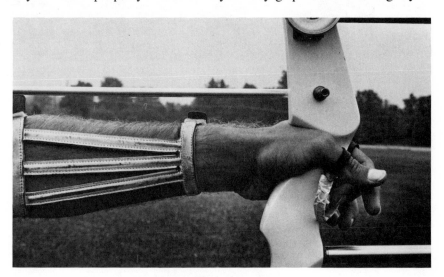

Straight wrist position

BOW ARM ELBOW

The only factors of concern here are proper string clearance and locking the elbow. Rotating the elbow out before you lock will guarantee best string clearance, especially upon a bad release that forces the string into the elbow. If this happens, you'll simply have to turn the elbow out more, or shoot with a more open stance. But if your bow

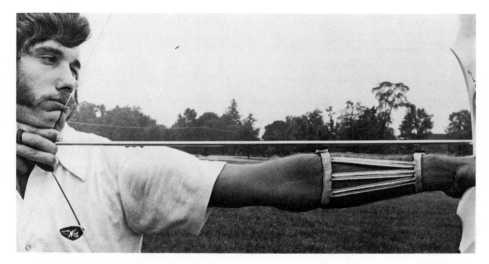

Bow arm elbow

arm is constructed in such a way that a bad release doesn't strike it when it's not rolled out, fine. *As long as the elbow is locked.* A very few archers have what is known as a "hyper-extended" elbow; with the elbow rolled and locked, the top of the elbow joint is actually higher than the remainder of their arm. This is not a matter for concern; it is simply a physical difference.

BOW SHOULDER

Low Shoulder

Pro: Shoulder is placed low and back in predraw position. Both shoulders are parallel to the ground. With this position you can better feel the pull in your back muscles; you get good string clearance and strong follow-through. It is a position that can be duplicated easily and exactly.

Con: A poorly conditioned archer may have trouble maintaining this shoulder, especially over long periods of shooting. The shoulder will rise and hunch, causing a shorter draw and low arrows. An archer un-

Low shoulder, side view

Low shoulder, front view

aware of good shoulder placement may set his shoulder down and back on one shot, high and back the next time.

High Shoulder

Pro: The shoulder is rotated forward and seated into the shoulder socket. It is a natural position for the shoulder to take under tension and can be duplicated consistently during long shooting periods because it is already in a "tired" position. It is a strong position for the casual shooter and a natural position for the heavy bow shooter.

Con: However, it creates minimal string clearance and a loss in positive back tension. The archer will push the bow arm forward upon release and may not develop a clean follow-through.

The most comfortable position may be somewhere between these two. You want to seat the shoulder low and back and then rotate it slightly forward until you feel the tension flowing smoothly from your locked bow arm into the shoulder socket. It will be strong, with good string clearance, and aid proper back tension and follow-through.

High shoulder, side view

High shoulder, front view

ANCHORING AIDS

Kisser Button

The kisser button adds a positive check for proper head attitude on every shot. It thus helps control the draw length, reminds the archer to keep teeth together, and adds confidence to the anchor.

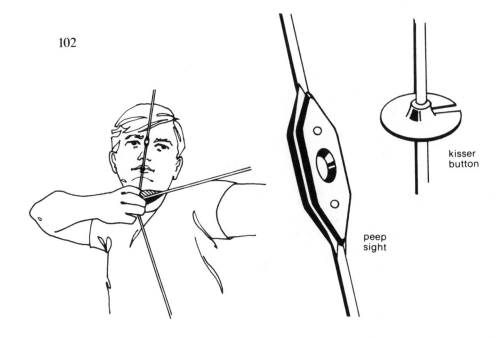

kisser
button

peep
sight

Archer using kisser button and peep sight

Peep Sight

This is another item that helps control proper head attitude, positions the anchor for fine aiming, makes proper string alignment easier, and creates better vision on target—thus increasing concentration and adding confidence.

These two aids help correct several faults: opening and closing the mouth, which causes high/low arrows; moving head toward string, which causes shorter draw length; floating anchor; changing head angle; overdrawing; failure to align string; failure to relax face and neck muscles on each shot.

AIMING HINTS

The aiming process should take 7 to 14 seconds. Do not move vision between sight and target while aiming; you will lose concentration and your eyes will tire. Maintain proper back tension during aiming and alignment. Concentrate on aiming and back tension when the sight settles on the target center. Concentrate on the middle of the center. Release only when alignment is correct and you are ready.

Let down and start over if something feels wrong. You do not need to shoot that arrow the first time you draw it; but you must be aware of the allotted time per end. If the sight picture isn't right, your form feels off, your concentration slackens, or you over-hold, then let down.

Aiming is only as good as the form controlling it. If you have refined your form to a consistent, almost subconscious effort, then you can properly concentrate on the proper aspects of each shot.

PHYSICAL CONTROLS

Breath Control

This is an important part of shooting that many shooters overlook. With proper breath control you can hold at full draw longer and shoot with less fatigue, which obviously will help your consistency and confidence.

For proper breath control, take a deep breath and exhale as you nock the arrow. Take another deep breath and exhale as you place string fingers and bow hand in proper position. Take the final deep breath and exhale to a comfortable feeling during predraw. Draw and maintain that comfortable feeling without exhaling or inhaling through the follow-through.

Eye Control

Proper eye control will aid your follow-through. It is a conscious effort to keep your eye in alignment and focus on the target until the arrow hits.

You should not see the arrow fly to the target. If you do, you are peeking, either by moving your head to left or right of the bow, or by moving your bow sideways. You may also be dropping your bow arm down out of the line of vision. Peeking and dropping the bow arm do not create accuracy.

You can achieve good eye control by relaxing your face and neck muscles, almost staring at the target with a blank expression.

COMPLETING THE SHOT

The shot is not completed when you release the arrow. Physically, you must follow through properly. Mentally, you review the total shot sequence, noting whichever repair or repairs you need to make on the next shot. You note this definitely—and positively—in your mind, and then you relax before beginning to prepare for the next shot sequence.

SHOOTING AT AN EMPTY TARGET WITH EYES CLOSED. Shooting at a close range (8-12 feet), with your eyes closed, at a large, empty target, is excellent practice to develop your shooting form. Since there is no target face to aim at, you should shut your eyes and concentrate solely on form. With your eyes shut, your sensory perception of shooting form heightens and you do not have the distraction of the scoring rings. If you were to shoot with eyes open, you would almost invariably soon begin selecting a definite spot on the empty target to aim at. The close distance and large target are safety measures.

This helps you develop a rhythm of strength and confidence. It is a positive approach that helps you understand your shot and keeps your mind from wandering. It simply increases your concentration.

TUNING YOUR BOW

You have a new bow and supposedly matched equipment. With this Super-Streak, Never-Miss Zinger bow, you are going to sweep all competition. But how do you go about fine tuning everything to ensure that sweep?

Eye control should give you relaxed face and neck muscles, almost staring at the target with a blank expression.

First, you must realize that there is no *one* exact way to tune a bow. Rather than getting into an argument with three friends who have three recommended procedures complete with half a dozen secret tricks guaranteed to succeed, decide on a simple, step-by-step methodology.

Before you begin adjusting equipment, be sure your form is consistent. If it is not, the equipment will react differently from different breakdowns in form.

If your form is set, do the shooting and tuning yourself. No one else can do it for you, because no one else will shoot that bow like you. But you should have an observer to confirm that each shot is consistent in form.

First read the manufacturer's recommendations. Be sure your arrows are the correct spine and length for that bow in your hands. Shoot the bow until it feels right in the general brace height area recommended. There will be about a ⅝-inch span in acceptable brace height, which will give fluidness of bow action with least amount of noise and maximum smoothness.

Then choose what seems to be the minimum acceptable brace height. Shoot a couple of ends at this height. Now go up for turns on the bowstring and shoot a couple more ends. Do this until you have reached the maximum acceptable brace height. You now know at *exactly* which height the bow performs with least noise and most smoothness. Set that proper brace height and mark it on paper. (Many archers like to mark brace height, nocking point height, and other pertinent data on a small piece of paper or tape affixed to their bow. The vital data is thus always available.)

To set nocking point, start ⅛ of an inch above 90 degrees. Wrap a piece of tape on the serving to serve as a nocking point locator.

Set Up Bow
1. String positioned down center of limbs.
2. Sight mounted parallel to the center of bow or string.
3. Cushion plunger set so arrow is on center line of bow.
4. Adjust sight so tip of sight pin is over center of arrow shaft.
5. Mark your shooting position so all arrows are shot from the same distance.

Set Nocking Point
1. You need three fletched arrows and one unfletched arrow, which will be called the "tuning arrow."
2. Shooting distance should be six yards (or meters).
3. Shoot fletched arrows to establish a group. Draw a circle around arrows and withdraw arrows from target.

4. Shoot tuning arrow. If the arrow strikes below the circle, move the nocking point down. If the arrow strikes above the circle, move the nocking point up. When the tuning arrow strikes at the same elevation as the circle, the nocking point position on the string is correct.

Set Cushion Plunger

1. Shoot fletched arrows to reestablish a group. Draw a circle around arrows and withdraw arrows from target.
2. Shoot tuning arrow. If tuning arrow strikes to the left of the circle, the arrow is flying stiff. Loosen the cushion plunger spring. If tuning arrow strikes to the right of the circle, the arrow is flying weak, i.e., acting as if it is underspined. Tighten the cushion plunger spring.
3. Repeat 2 until tuning arrow strikes in the circle.

When you determine the proper nocking point height for shooting the arrows straight into the target on the vertical axis, mark the serving and affix the nocking point locator firmly.

The arrow rest must be directly above the pressure point of your grip on the handle.

If you're using a button (cushion plunger, also known as panic button), be sure the arrow makes contact directly in the center of the button and the center of the shaft. This will give even tension on the button and produce the proper effect on the arrow.

If the arrow appears to be too light-spined with the lightest spring

10–30 yards bare shaft test for nocking point location
3 fletched arrows
1 bare shaft
(right-handed archer)

Nocking Point
too low; raise
nocking point

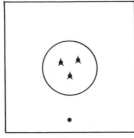

Nocking Point
too high; lower
nocking point

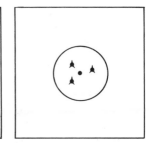

Nocking point
is correct

in the button, go to a heavier-spined arrow—there's nothing more the button can do. If the arrow is too heavy with the heaviest spring in the button, drop down an arrow size or (if you're using aluminum) try a thinner-walled shaft of the same diameter.

An arrow that remains with nock left of center (right-handed archer) in the target is spined too weak. An arrow nock remaining right of center is spined too strong. The reverse is true for a left-handed archer.

The proper arrow rest should give a cushion support to the arrow, not a rigid support. It must give downward, although very slightly, such as a flexible plastic or a spring rest. This is very important if you are not shooting with a pressure button. Talk it over with a pro and try a few rests until you find the one that works best for you.

You cannot tune for vertical and horizontal alignment simultaneously. Check the nocking point height first.

The more stabilizing weight you place on the bow, the more torque and vibrations it will absorb to smooth out the shot. Conversely, you do not want too much weight, because this will begin affecting bow performance. You will not get the proper snap out of the limbs, because the added weight seems to absorb this.

The proper stabilizer will balance the bow basically upright upon release. A bow that tips forward will catch the back of the arrow. The bow should remain upright so it jumps at the target upon release.

Various positions of stabilizers will affect groups. Experimentation will show you which works best for you.

Looseness or firmness of the stabilizer attachment will also affect grouping. If the stabilizers are too loose, they may exaggerate the torque in your hand or they may react so slowly that they won't have any stabilizing effect because the limbs have already delivered the arrow.

If one stabilizer is too loose and one is too tight, they will affect an arrow unequally. There is a controversy over whether one should be tighter or looser than another. The general feeling is that the tighter one will absorb bow vibrations faster, so it should be on the stronger limb to equalize the limbs. My experience has been that it doesn't seem to make much difference as long as they are fairly close together and relatively firm.

Counterbalances must be very firm.

To check for vane clearance, sprinkle talcum or baby powder on the arrow plate above the arrow rest and across the entire bow window and shelf. Hold the bow horizontal, arrow rest up, and snap the string lightly. This seems to vibrate the powder more firmly onto the surface. Blow off the residue.

Now shoot a few arrows and see what needs adjusting on the arrow rest and/or nocking point. If you tuned everything properly with the bare shaft, you should have little or no problems.

Here are some additional checkpoints for fine tuning: feather or vane size; string size (number of strands); fit of nocks on string; handle shape (if it doesn't fit you properly you will shoot inconsistently); amount of window cutout; length of bow relative to string angle at full draw; limb alignment and tiller.

SETTING UP ONE PERFECT SHOT

I approach the line with a *positive* attitude, straddle the line, find the foot position and stance that allow me to be the most comfortable, and then relax. (If you're shooting indoors, you may want to use a pencil and mark your foot positions so you will stand in exactly the same position every time.)

Now I'm on the line, resting the bow tip on my shoe, looking at the gold, already beginning the concentration on that spot. Many times I won't even take my eyes off the gold to reach into my quiver for an arrow.

I pull the arrow from the quiver and put it on the bow, snapping the nock onto the string. If I am at this point still concentrating on the gold—and I should be—I will check that I've nocked the arrow correctly by just brushing my thumb up to where the cock fletch should be. If it's there, fine. If it isn't, it doesn't upset the sequence; I just turn the arrow around. This checking has become such a natural habit that I don't really know I'm doing it, and I can continue concentrating on the spot.

From there, I relax my concentration on the target. I pick the bow up off my shoe, just lifting the handle, now worrying about hand position. I put the tab on the string and find the most comfortable place on the string for my fingers. (For me this is just forward of the

PERFECT SHOT SEQUENCE: Beginning the concentration on gold . . .

Placing the string fingers comfortably . . .

joint nearest the fingertip; for you it may be deeper or not as deep, depending on your personal preference. Use whichever style gives you best performance.)

While I am doing this I have brought my knees slightly forward so they are not locked, but I am still standing up straight. (Locked knees make it difficult to keep your balance; you have a tendency to rock forward or back. You must maintain some muscular tension in the legs to maintain balance, and locking the knees takes away that proper tension.)

At this point, I have already put into the back of my mind the checkpoints of stance, finger position on string, nocking the arrow, and leg position. These are four checkpoints I need not worry about again unless I take the arrow down at some point and have to start the sequence over.

Bringing concentration back to the target . . .

Now I bring my concentration back up to the target, and while extending the bow arm, I seat my hand into the bow—comfortably re-

Extending the bow arm fully, rolling the elbow out, dropping the bow shoulder into place and locking it there . . .

laxed and at a pressure point directly underneath the arrow rest. I check this visually, and by how the hand position feels on the handle. (Some archers mark a spot on their bow just below the shelf and a spot on the V of their thumb and hand, and line up the two marks.)

As I extend the bow arm, I extend it fully and roll my elbow at the same time, in addition to dropping the bow shoulder into place and locking it there. At this point I have come to what is a ''predraw'' or ''half draw'' position, since my drawing hand is still inches away from my face. I have my drawing hand thumb extended toward my bow

Beginning to settle the sight on the gold, even before reaching full draw . . .

shoulder. The thumb is a checkpoint to insure that the bow shoulder is, in fact, locked down. If the shoulder is up, and not locked, my thumb will actually brush or touch the shoulder.

At this point I am settling the sight on the gold, even though I'm only at half draw. This is a more positive approach than settling the sight on a point just outside the gold and coming into it. I'm also mentally and physically checking by feel the finger pressure on the string,

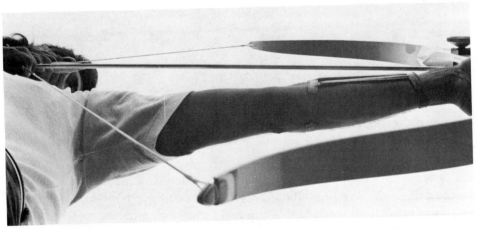

Checking alignment of bow hand, wrist, elbow, and shoulder . . .

the alignment of the bow hand, wrist, elbow, and shoulder. From this point, I put into the back of my mind the checkpoints of finger pressure on the string, bow hand position, elbow rolled down, and shoulder locked down. They are all locked into the proper position, and should not change.

Now I again take my concentration away from the target and put it onto the clicker, and begin the second half of the draw. From this point on, until I'm actually settled at full draw, I won't bring my concentration to the sight or target. I watch the clicker and draw the arrow back until the string contacts the lower part of my chin. At this point, I try to set the clicker as far down the slope of the point, toward the tip, as possible. From here I slide the string up my chin until the forefinger of the drawing hand touches the inside of the jawbone and the base of the chin. (I also tighten up my tongue muscle, so the finger touches it first, then relax it as I come up into the jawbone. This just gives me another reference point.)

As the string contacts the lower part of the chin, set the clicker as far down the slope of the point, toward the tip, as possible . . .

Now I am mentally and physically checking how the anchor feels, how high my drawing elbow is, how my head position is, how the clicker is still set on the arrow tip, and I start concentrating on slightly increasing my back tension. If everything feels right at this point I will move my concentration and eye focus to the target and bring the sight, which appears slightly fuzzy because it is out of focus, to the center of the target. As soon as the sight actually settles on the middle of the target, I will put more and more concentration into increasing my back tension, in addition to trying to force the sight to stay in the middle of the target.

Slide the string up until the forefinger of the drawing hand touches the inside of the jawbone and the base of the chin . . .

Because I'm concentrating on increasing back tension, I have set up a pull to bring the arrow from underneath the clicker. When the clicker actually clicks, I react as though it were a trigger to reach a peak of concentration, which keeps that sight and my eyes pushed into the gold—and at the same time increases my back tension even more as I relax my fingers to release the arrow. This will keep my bow arm up, and it takes only a split second to accomplish all this.

The triggering of more concentration on the back tension sets up a natural follow-through, in the sense that the back muscles will draw the hand back into the follow-through position. Then I hold this position for a few seconds while I make whatever mental corrections need to be made, and finally I put the bow back down.

Everyone has basically this same system of checking. However, different individuals, due to different mental and physical setups, will

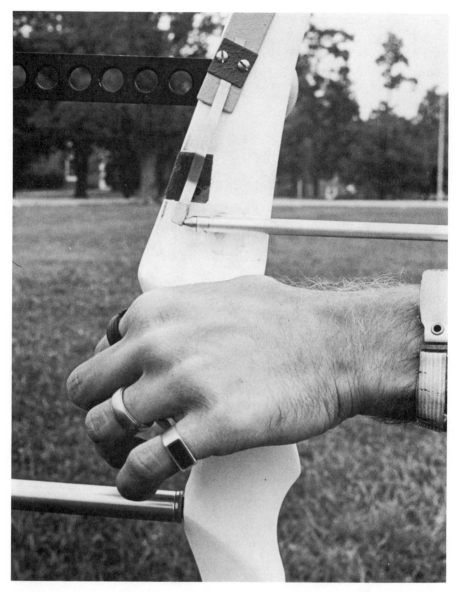

With the clicker set, check the anchor feel, drawing elbow height, and head position; begin concentrating on slightly increasing back tension . . .

With properly developed back tension, when the arrow is pulled from underneath the clicker the archer will be triggered to shoot at the moment of peak concentration and aim . . .

The triggering of more concentration on back tension in the final moment of draw sets up a natural follow-through, which is held for a few moments as the archer evaluates the shot and makes mental corrections, if needed.

concentrate on different points of the building of a shot sequence. If a person has had trouble with release, he will concentrate more on different aspects of the release. This also applies to the bow hand, or any other part of the sequence. This is natural, for some parts of the shot are easy for certain people, while others may have difficulty with that part. Consequently, you will not need to concentrate as much on the easy aspects as on the difficult parts; however, no one will ignore checking the easy parts, because a complete check must be made each time to be sure the shot is set up properly.

This helps create the necessary positive mental attitude. Use the easy parts, the natural strengths, as the basic building blocks for your shot sequence. Then work on your difficult parts of the shot to bring them *up* to the skilled level of your easy parts. You know each shot must be a duplication of the previous shot. So work for a completely developed form, always bringing up the weak points.

At this stage of skill development, you know what must be done to improve certain elements of your shot. Do *not* tell yourself, or let a coach tell you, "This is wrong, or that is wrong." Instead, tell yourself, "I know how the bow shoulder must be set and locked, so I'll work to do it right once. Then I'll duplicate it."

You're now working from confidence and strength, not from distracting worry.

chapter six

arrow patterns—what they tell you about your form

Despite what you may often think, an arrow does not have a mind of its own. It will only go where you, through your shooting form and your handling of the bow, direct it.

So, if you've been shooting archery long enough to develop relative consistency in your performance, your arrow groupings can tell you a lot about your form—what your strengths are and what your weaknesses may be. Unfortunately, groupings off center of target don't shout out, "Hey, you're doing this and this and this right, so keep it up, fella." They have their own subtle positive indicators—mainly in the fact that you're grouping your arrows, which means consistency of some kind.

Their direct message is what you're doing *wrong;* you can see this because the group of arrows is off center. This seems a bit unfortunate at times, because we prefer to stress the *positive* aspects of your personal archery shooting form. But if you accept the grouping patterns as a not-so-subtle reminder of the particular parts of your form that need work, then you'll make the corrections with the right frame of mind.

Only four patterns are given here. We did not use a "scattered arrows'' pattern because such results can indicate a host of errors, the main one being that the archer scattering his arrows has not yet developed consistency in shooting form and has not really reached a level of skill at which he can make full value of the arrow pattern evaluations shown here.

The left and right patterns shown here are for right-handed archers. Left-handed archers should simply reverse the indicators.

When checking your grouping, before analyzing your form check all equipment tuning. Your form may be great, but your equipment setup could be letting you down.

high strike pattern

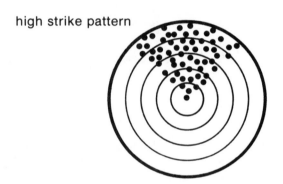

HIGH ARROW PATTERN

- Bow hand low on bow handle, increasing stress on lower limb. This builds up extra stored energy in the lower limb, which lifts arrow on release.

- Bow hand grip more relaxed than usual. Permits bow to jump forward in hand on release more than normal, giving more efficient shot.

- Bow arm lifted on release.

- Bow arm extended more than normal. Increases draw length and draw weight. Secondary result is some left error.

- Bow shoulder extended farther than normal, which increases draw.

- Drawing hand thrown back on release, fingers jerked off string. Often accompanied by head position being back too far.

- Pinching down on arrow.

- String plucking and peeking, done together. Also tends to throw arrows left.

- Finger pressure on string is uneven, with more pulling from bottom finger. Increases stored energy in lower limb. Usually related to elbow position being too high.

- Flicking fingers down on release, due to drag on fingers, which pulls string and nock down.

- Uneven release of finger pressure with lower finger leaving string last.

- Chin pulled down from normal head position, lowering the anchor.

- Mouth open, if usually closed—lowers anchor position.

- Head too far back, increases draw length.

- Letting anchor (under-the-chin) drift off outside of chin to the right, tends to increase draw length. Also causes left arrow.

- Pushing bow arm as a unit (including bow shoulder, arm, and hand) forward upon release.

- Low drawing arm elbow, pulls anchor down. Usually found with corner-of-mouth anchor.

- Failure to compensate for strong tailwind.

- Bowsight setting too low (raises arrow rest).

- Nocking point too low.

- Arrow rest improperly placed, points up.

- Nocks not on straight, point up at end.

- Lower bow limb too stiff.

- Arrow lighter in physical weight than others. This is more an individual arrow error than a grouping trait.

- Too little spiral on fletching, does not create enough drag.

- String height too low; string stays with arrow longer, delivers more energy.
- Weight variations in tips, more of an individual arrow error.
- Shooting faster than normal.
- Aimed high.
- Overdrawn arrow, arrow too short. Sometimes also shows in left/right error.

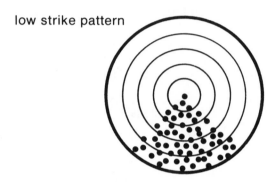

low strike pattern

LOW ARROW PATTERN

- Squeezing bow usually puts extra stress on top limb, causes it to recover faster. If you normally have a loose grip, squeezing will inhibit action of bow, reducing cast.
- High wrist, if not normal style.
- Dropping bow arm on release. Often includes left/right error.
- Bent bow arm, shortening draw and reducing bow cast.
- Improper bow shoulder seating and tension allows shoulder to rise backward, shortening draw.
- Chest collapse, causes loss of back tension.
- Anticipation of release in a relaxation of back muscles, which allows drawing hand to move forward rapidly, but often almost imperceptibly, before release.

- Dead or static release.
- High drawing arm elbow (with corner-of-mouth anchor).
- Improper tension on base and second knuckles of drawing hand. Also causes some left arrows.
- Fingers and back of hand not in straight line with forearm. Also causes some left arrows through plucking.
- Creeping forward from full anchor, or not coming to full final anchor point before release.
- Peeking, or raising head on release.
- Head dropped forward during anchor and release, shortens draw.
- Dropping bow arm upon release.
- Arrow rest improperly placed so arrow slides down rest before release. Also causes some left arrows.
- Improper arrow clearance off rest, fletches strike rest.
- Arrow rest too close to shelf, fletches strike shelf. Also causes right arrow.
- String striking body, clothes, or armguard.
- Shooting through clicker (failure to develop full power of bow and not enough back tension).
- Arrow nocking point too high.
- Stiff upper limb of bow.
- Arrow tips too heavy, also creating right error because of spine change.
- Worn feather fletching.
- Too much spiral on fletching, causes excess drag.
- Worn tab, with ridge in permanent set. Also causes left error.
- Brace height too high.
- Nocks out of line, point down at end.
- Arrow moves up string during draw and release.

right strike pattern

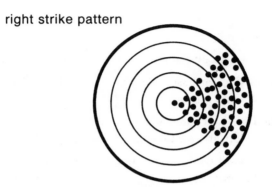

RIGHT ARROW PATTERN

- Hand pressure point too far left on bow handle—causes torque.
- Canting bow to right on top limb.
- Looking inside of string (between string and bow), creating improper alignment.
- Bow arm moving to right upon release.
- Wrist breaks left on release.
- Plucking string on release.
- Leaning body forward, tendency to continue leaning upon release.
- Incorrect estimation of left-to-right wind.
- Shooting under clicker.
- Sight set too far right.
- Nock too tight on string.
- Nock points right at end.
- Fletching striking arrow rest.
- Rest placed too far in, with properly spined arrow.
- Brace height too low, increased string oscillation.
- Recurves twisted right.
- Arrow strikes inside edge of bow window.

- Arrow spine too soft.
- Arrow rest too far forward or back of adjustable pressure point (button).

left strike pattern

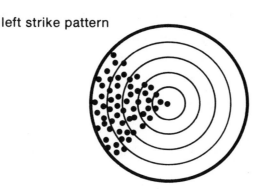

LEFT ARROW PATTERN

- Bow hand too far right on handle.
- Canting bow to left on top limb.
- Wrist breaking right on release.
- Pushing with bow arm; also produces high arrow.
- Bow shoulder set to left.
- Plucking string on release.
- Looking outside of string, with string aligned farther right than usual. (Using target and sight pin as center of alignment.)
- Improper back tension, not fully developed draw—causes pluck. And low arrow.
- Failure to reach full draw and anchor. Also causes low error.
- Head pushed forward, moves anchor right off body and bow line. Also causes low arrow.
- Leaning body backward, parallel to shooting line.
- Striking clothes or armguard. Also causes low arrow.

- Aimed too far left.
- Collapse on release. Also causes low arrow.
- Shooting through clicker.
- Nock too tight on string, with too high a string height.
- Nock out of line, pointing left at back.
- Arrow sliding off rest. Also causes low arrow.
- Limb twisted left.
- Arrow rest too far out, with properly spined arrow.
- Spine too stiff.
- Too light a point (if using weighted points) in relation to other points.
- Arrow rest positioned too far forward or back of pressure point (button) on bow handle.

chapter seven

basic questions

How do I build good shooting form?

In any sport, you want the basics to be as easy as possible. In archery, you must learn to utilize the minimum amount of effort necessary, using the fewest number of muscles needed for the least possible time necessary to make a controlled, positive shot. This is done with the basic "T" body form and stance. You should have the bones of arms and shoulder in line for the least amount of muscular effort. And when you're properly lined up, you can relax many muscles, which helps considerably in making a good shot. Any time your form strays from the basic "T," you are using extra, and incorrect, muscle tension to hold your form.

How do I make sure my bow arm elbow is rolled out of the way of the string path?

You basically solve it by trial and error. As a basic check, when you're learning to shoot, you can extend your bow arm, roll the elbow down and out, and then fold your arm toward your chest. If your elbow is

The basic "T" of body form and stance.

rolled properly, your bow hand will strike you squarely in the chest. Advanced archers usually check bow elbow during predraw, making sure the inside of the elbow is vertical. This is a conscious effort, sometimes almost forcing the elbow down out of the way.

How do I solve a bow shoulder that's rolled in too far or too high?

This form weakness causes variations in draw because the shoulder is not locked and creeps up. This forces you to use extra muscles, instead of locking it down into the shoulder joint. If you roll it in too far, you don't get proper string clearance on shoulder or elbow.

Bow shoulder is incorrectly rolled in too far and too high.

To correct this, either establish your predraw position higher, so your shoulder will seat downward and hopefully lock in proper position, and/or lean slightly toward the target, which will also help keep the bow shoulder down. Opening the stance slightly will give more shoulder clearance (if you're unable to solve the problem through corrected shoulder seating). If your bow shoulder is a drastic problem, push your head slightly forward over your chest; this also gives more string clearance.

How do I keep my bow hand from sliding in too far or out too far on the bow handle?

One good method to correct this error is to establish predraw position higher so shoulder seats downward and hopefully locks in proper position. Other solutions are explained in the text.

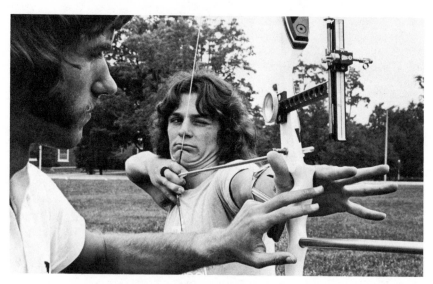

To solidify proper hand position, establish the proper lifeline of the hand through the wrist and then into the forearm, elbow, and shoulder. Do not spread the fingers this far because it can cause your wrist to collapse. Fingers should be loosely curled in front of the grip.

If you get too far in, you will have too little string clearance; if you're too far out on the thumb (as opposed to a more proper position on the meat of the hand at the base of the thumb), you will get some right bow torque and a very tired hand trying to hold that draw weight pressure.

To correct, move your hand position the proper direction to put the lifeline of the hand along the main part of the handle and wrist directly behind it, so the weight of the bow is flowing from the hand into the wrist into the elbow and then into the shoulder in a straight line along the bones of this unit. For extra assurance, mark your bow on the shelf directly above the main pressure point on the handle and mark the main pressure point on your hand. Then vertically align the marks.

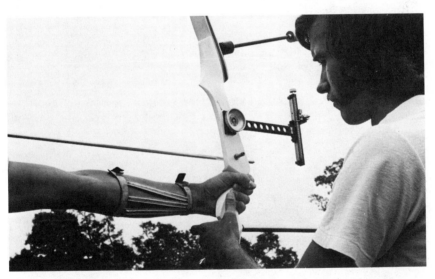

This bow is gripped too hard and can also cause the wrist to collapse.

Why do I seem to grip the bow too hard?

Simply because you're afraid of dropping it. When most archers begin shooting, they fail to realize that it's possible to relax the fingers around the bow handle. In shooting, the bow will jump forward into the fingers and give better performance. The weight and resistance of your fingers

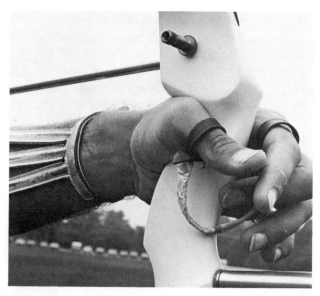

A finger sling will add confidence and let you grip the bow in the proper loose manner. This will allow the bow to jump forward properly in your hand upon release of the arrow.

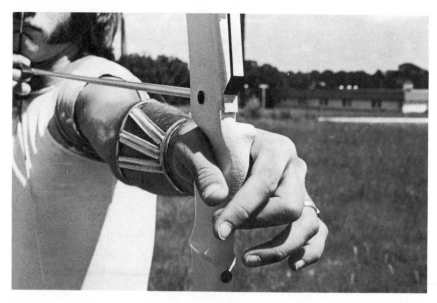

This is a loose, but confident, grip without the finger sling. The bow can react properly upon the shot, but will not be dropped.

will stop the bow safely. Some archers partially solve this problem: they relax the fingers, but then grab the bow the instant of release.

If you tend to grab the bow, or hold it tightly, try a finger sling or bow sling. After a few shots, as you realize that the bow jumps into the sling, you'll gain confidence and relax your hand. If you can then discard the sling, fine. If you gain confidence and relax because of the sling's presence, by all means continue using it. The hand *must* be relaxed, because any time you put tension in your bow hand, there is the possibility that you won't put in the same tension every time. And every time you use a muscle, the human fallibility means you may not use it the same way twice. But you must, because in archery you are seeking perfect uniformity shot after shot.

How do I develop a strong anchor, yet keep the hand relaxed?

You have to relax the fingers so your hand can act almost independently of the wrist. This is so the fingers can turn and twist slightly to fit properly against the jawbone instead of following the hand rigidly. You need to get your hand—especially the base knuckles—underneath the jawbone for a firm, consistent anchor.

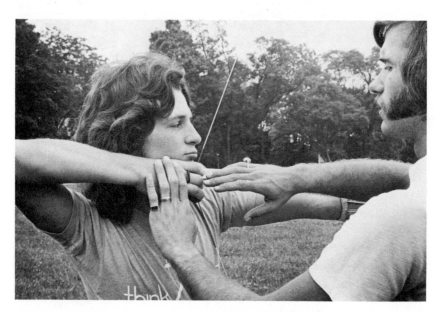

This drawing hand is not relaxed properly in the base knuckles, so it will tend to curl inward, almost wrapping around the string in extreme cases.

Archers with short or heavy hands have trouble getting underneath or on the line of the jawbone, mainly because they usually grip the string with too much actual finger tension, almost wrapping the whole hand around the string.

Any time the hand sits on the point of the chin, you have only one reference point to form a good, solid anchor. That's why you need the solid base of the entire jawbone line. The more you pull your drawing elbow back, the more you'll find your drawing hand seats in closer and closer to the neck. Ideally, the whole ridge from the first knuckle of the top finger all the way back to the base knuckle and wrist should be on your jawbone or touching it in some way. As you learn to relax the fingers so they work independently of your drawing hand and arm, try to turn the base knuckles in toward your neck as much as possible so they will slip underneath the jawbone.

Properly pulled back, the drawing hand seats closer to the neck and under the jawbone.

Any time the knuckle and finger ride on the jawbone, you get an inconsistent anchor. It can ride up and out or down and in. Up and out gives low, left arrows; down and in causes high, right arrows because of the changing level of anchor point and string alignment.

What causes me to pinch the arrow off the string?

Too much tension in the first finger, with the second finger riding too close to the bottom of the nock. When you draw and start placing more tension on the string, you pull more with the top finger, and the second finger changes the angle of the string at the finger contact point. This will raise the arrow up off the arrow rest in a direct vertical manner.

Correct this by moving out slightly toward the end of the finger on the top finger, or take a less deep grip with the top finger. Also, spread the fingers slightly away from the nock.

Why do I twist the arrow off the rest?

This is caused by trying to pull too much with the fingers instead of the back. After you reach full anchor, or even before, the arrow falls off

A top finger seated too deeply, caused by a high elbow or too deep a grip at the beginning, can cause you to pinch the arrow off the string, apply improper tension on the string, and give you sore fingers. Correct this by moving slightly toward end of top finger, lowering elbow to proper height, and spreading fingers slightly. (See preceding photo.)

because you're starting to pull inward with the fingers, rather than letting the string roll slightly toward the tips of the fingers.

Correct this by relaxing the fingers more, or by placing them on the string at a 90-degree angle to the arrow. As you begin the draw and bring your hand around to proper alignment with the arrow, the string will twist slightly and pull the arrow into the rest and against the window. Be sure you twist only the string; do not pinch the nock because this will apply too much pressure to the arrow and ruin the shot. You should also use snap-on nocks, which will help keep the arrow on the string whether fingers contact the nock or not.

How do I solidify an erratic bow arm?

This is caused by not holding the sight on the target center through release and follow-through. Some archers, in trying to peek or shoot more dynamically, will push the bow arm forward.

Corrections could be as simple as being sure that you aim completely through the shot, not only using eye/target contact, but eye/sight/target contact. Try to keep the sight on the center, or as close to center as possible, until the arrow strikes the target.

A rare cause can be a bow that is simply physically too heavy to hold at proper height with arm extended. Then you need a bow with lighter physical weight.

How do I correct a bad release?

First, determine the cause. This could be too low a drawing elbow, elbow too far out from proper alignment, not enough back tension, or too much finger tension.

Too low an elbow means you are using some of the muscles in the lower part of the shoulder and underarm to pull your elbow down. When you do this, you take away a lot of the tension that should be going into the back and shoulder muscles. This will cause high arrows, mainly because in pulling the elbow down, upon release of arrow and tension, the muscles are still reacting in a downward motion, which pulls the elbow and arm and fingers down instead of back. You will also get a slightly dead release.

The correction is to bring your drawing elbow up slightly, relax the muscles underneath the drawing arm as much as possible and just try to increase back tension around the shoulder blade area.

A drawing elbow too far out of alignment can be caused by a draw length that's shorter than it should be, which pulls the elbow forward, or you may simply have a short forearm. This physical characteristic simply keeps you from getting the elbow properly back in line when your fingers reach the correct anchor position.

A draw length shorter than it should be can cause the drawing elbow to be too far out of alignment. This will also put improper strain on the shoulder muscles and not develop enough back tension.

To correct the problem of improperly short draw length, be sure you set as deep an anchor as possible, without twisting your head, and concentrate more on developing proper back tension. This will pull your elbow back properly. Do not place the drawing tension in your shoulder, because this will not allow you to reach proper draw length, and the shoulder will tire quickly. This leads to collapse, and other problems.

You might also need to shoot a longer arrow, which will allow you to develop the proper alignment without changing head positions.

Improper finger tension (pulling with the fingers) lets you allow the back muscles to relax, or maybe not function at all. You pull by doubling up the fingers. In doing so, you usually lose a little of either anchor point or alignment of string; you will also get a slightly dead release and a pluck, because the fingers cannot relax fast enough to get out of the way of the string on release. The less tension you have in your drawing fingers the better, because they will relax faster and get rid of the string more cleanly. Just be sure you do not allow your wrist to relax out of proper alignment with the arrow and forearm when you relax the fingers.

Proper back tension should flow in the direction the coach's fingers are pointing and be felt by the muscles in the shoulder blade area.

Improper back tension is caused by a number of things, but usually by laziness. A person's subconscious decides it would rather take it easy and hold the string, rather than actually working and pulling the string. This can cause a very dead release, because there is no tension being exerted in a backward motion. When the string is released, the back does not draw the release hand into the proper follow-through position. So you cure this by simply trying to transfer more of the work into the muscles surrounding the shoulder blade, concentrating on back tension while you aim.

What does it mean if the leading hip is cocked toward the target?

You're actually leaning backward from the hips, probably because you're using a bow with too heavy a draw weight. When you lean back, even though you may stay in proper alignment, you usually shorten your draw length because the bow shoulder has a tendency to rise and come back as you lean. This can also cause a lack of back tension; you are exerting so much tension in the lower back to hold your shoulder from rising even more that the muscles in your upper back cannot perform as well.

A cocked hip means you're actually leaning backward from the hips, which can lead to several breakdowns in form.

How does brace height affect bow performance?

It affects bow cast. With a lower brace height (in effect, a longer string) the string will push the arrow longer, and thus faster, because it must move farther to allow the limbs to recover properly. Higher brace height gives less speed because the string does not travel as far when the limbs recover. Brace height also affects, for a given set of matched arrows, the grouping of those arrows.

Always check for proper brace height before you begin shooting; improper brace height causes the bow to perform poorly.

Find a given ½'' or ⅝'' range of brace height where the bow performs best. Within this range, you will get good arrow groups. You will also find at least a four- or five-yard difference in cast between the low height and the high height.

You will also find that a bow performs smoother and quieter within this good area of brace height. Somewhere along the line in fine tuning your bow, you usually have to sacrifice a little of one or two of these points (smoothness, speed, quietness) when you find the exact brace height that performs best. This is because the lower height produces speed, but higher brace heights produce smoothness and quietness (the string is more taut and produces less slap on the recurve).

What, exactly, is "tiller"?

It's how strong or weak the limbs are in relation to each other. When you measure bow tiller, you measure the difference in distance between given points on both limbs to the string. The difference is the tiller. Generally, the lower limb has more tension than the top limb because most people shoot with a low wrist, which exerts more pressure on the bottom limb. Yet, the limbs must recover together to produce a good shot.

What are the definitions of aggressive and nonaggressive shooters?

An aggressive shooter is a rhythm shooter. He makes things happen when he wants them to happen; he doesn't wait for them to happen. Aggressive shooters shoot more with the conscious mind, whereas nonaggressive shooters shoot slightly with the subconscious mind, in the sense that they are waiting for some signal to tell them when to shoot. The difference may be related to the dynamics. An aggressive shooter will expend a vast amount of energy over a short time to make the thing happen. The nonaggressive shooter will expend a little energy over a longer time waiting for something to happen, such as the moment when everything in his form and aiming comes to a stop with the sight pin on the center of the target. His subconscious will say "now" and he will release. The aggressive shooter will force his form and aiming to stop the sight pin on the center of the target, and when it does he will shoot. Both styles work. However, there are quite a few more aggressive than nonaggressive shooters.

Should I actually stop dead in movement at full anchor?

No, because the laws of force, energy, and mass decree that it's harder to start something moving than it is to keep it moving. If you actually stop pulling when you first attain full draw, it is much harder to start pulling again (to develop proper back tension) than it is to continue moving. *But this continual movement is almost imperceptible;* it's more sensory than visual. It may look, to a bystander, as though the shooter is not moving; but he actually is, however small that drawing hand/arm/shoulder movement may be.

You'll find that it is almost impossible to beat a rhythm shooter when he has the correct rhythm. This rhythm implies fluid motion; there is something happening all the time. He slows down at full draw, but he never really stops. Proper back tension will develop this fluid motion; the tension must be increasing constantly. There must be back tension to begin the draw, pull the hand into anchor, keep increasing back tension during the aim, and increase the back tension even more at the exact moment of release to bring the string fingers off the string quickly and smoothly and your back into the follow-through position.

What is a clicker and what does it do?

A clicker is a piece of spring steel attached to the side of the bow window, with the arrow going between the clicker and the bow. When the arrow is actually pulled back from underneath the clicker, the band snaps against the bow, making a clicking sound or setting up a faint vibration in the bow handle that the bowhand can feel.

It is used as a draw check and as a trigger. As a draw check, it insures that when the arrow is drawn to the point at which the clicker snaps against the bow, the arrow is in exactly the same draw length as previous arrows, so if other conditions are duplicated identically, the arrow should perform the same as all previous arrows.

Using the clicker as a trigger, the archer will release when he hears or feels the clicker snap. In addition to giving him the draw check, it tells him when to release. It thus insures that you have proper back tension at the moment of release, because you have to pull through it. This final pull is always performed after the aiming procedure has been initiated. You should not initiate the final pull until you feel you are

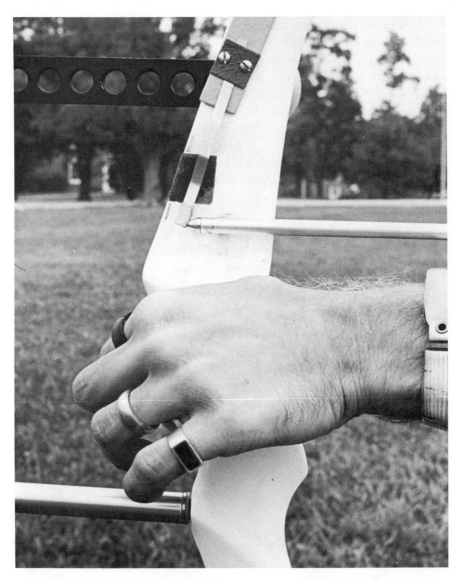

A clicker can serve as a draw check and as a trigger.

ready to shoot the arrow—YOU make that clicker click, and you can make it click anytime you want.

You cannot become a slave to a clicker if you make it do what you want it to, when you want it to.

If you have a visual draw check other than a clicker—such as just looking at the point of the arrow, or a line reference point on the bow—and also *if* you do not have a freezing problem, and *if* you can aim at the middle of the gold when you want it there, and *if* you can control your reactions enough that you only release when you want to, then you don't need a clicker. A nonaggressive shooter would be most likely to have satisfied all these conditions, and not need a clicker. Because of all these *ifs,* nonclicker shooters are more inclined to have up and down days than clicker shooters.

There are two main points of concern in shooting a clicker. (1) The positioning of the clicker on the arrow has to be as consistently close to the very tip of the arrow as you dare. The best place is within $\frac{1}{16}$'' to $\frac{1}{8}$''. (2) The final pull through the clicker must be controlled and proper. After you are all set up, aimed sufficiently, ready to actually shoot the arrow—but the clicker has not clicked—you must increase back tension to give you one, *and only one,* smooth, fast pull. When you make up your mind to shoot, you must say ''now'' and that clicker must click. You cannot start to pull, stop because the sight may have drifted off, then try to start again. This tends to create a creep and a less active release, because you have already expended so much energy in attempting to get through the clicker, that you don't have enough energy left to get your draw hand back through the follow-through.

You cannot pull nice and easy, so-o-o-o-o-o slow, through a clicker, because you end up with a static draw. It takes so much energy, over so long a time, that you are actually just holding and fighting the strain, not actually pulling.

How do you figure the wind?

When there is a 5-15 mph gusting wind, I set my sight for approximately 10 mph with the wind—a dead mean. When I feel it to be less or more—judging how the wind feels on me and the way the flags are blowing—I'll aim off this setting to properly compensate either farther right or farther left. And if there's suddenly no wind, I'll compensate slightly more toward the target. It's all a matter of experience, and of watching the flags *upwind* from your target—that's the wind that will be at your target when your arrow gets there.

I won't put down a shot if the wind changes. It is harder, and more expensive in time and energy, to let an arrow down than it is to shoot it. And who is to say, in a wind situation, that the wind won't be blowing more on the next shot? If you feel right, go ahead and aim corrected and shoot. As you practice in the wind, you will learn how your arrows shoot in the wind, how much they drift. Then it's up to you to determine aiming point at full draw while checking everything else.

Why do most target archers use plastic vanes instead of feathers?

They're more accurate because they are man-made rather than turkey-made. They are also less affected by wind, thinner, lower, and smoother-surfaced. This gives you more speed and less wind drift because the arrow is in the air a shorter length of time and the wind can't

Plastic vanes are used for most outdoor competitive shooting because they are more uniform than feathers, smoother, less affected by wind.

catch a vane like it can a feather. Also, feathers absorb water during rain and they lie down, which reduces their stabilizing value and speed of the arrow.

Is it advisable to change my stance when shooting in the wind?

I believe so. If you are shooting in a left-to-right wind, open your stance (right-handed shooter) so your body turns more into the wind. With a right-to-left wind, close it more. This makes your stance stronger, even though you are facing into the wind. This is not a big move, only an inch or so with the feet. But it is worthwhile, because it takes tremendous effort and time to bring an arrow back onto the gold when the wind is blowing against your body and bow arm.

Why attach the sight on the face of the bow?

It will create a larger degree of angle between the line of sight and the arrow, so the closer sight markings will be higher on the sight bar. This leaves more room at the bottom of the sight bar for longer distance markings.

Why attach the sight on the back of the bow?

The farther from your eye you position the sight pin, the finer an aiming piece it will become, simply because the pin is smaller to view and thus allows more critical aiming. This is the ideal indoor archery setting.

How would you explain archery in its simplest form?

Learn to make one perfect shot, and then be able to duplicate that shot time after time.

Why is it advantageous to practice at close distance on an empty bale with my eyes shut?

Because you concentrate solely on form. You develop smoothness because your mind and body tighten up when the eye and mind see an actual target to aim at and hit. With no target, there's nothing to aim at, so you don't tighten up.

Shooting at an empty target lets you concentrate on form development.

What happens if my feet are too close together in stance?

You simply lose the balance needed for stability. Your body sways. The strongest stance is with your feet placed shoulder-width apart or slightly more, with toes pointing slightly outward in a comfortable, natural position. This will help you balance more on the balls of your feet.

What difference does angle of fletching make on the arrow?

The smaller the degree of fletching, the less control exerted on the arrow; but there's also less wind resistance and the arrow thus flies faster. A higher degree of angle gives more control and more wind resistance, so the arrow will fly slower.

Proper stance, with feet about shoulder-width and toes turned out slightly, is strong, stable, and well-balanced.

How do weighted tips affect arrow spine?

They will weaken the spine slightly because there is more resistance at the tip, more mass to be put into motion by the string. The arrow bends more as it goes around the bow.

What's the difference in shooting with a pin sight or ring sight?

With a pin sight, you have a tendency to attempt to aim finer, tighten up more, and shoot a less perfect shot, although your aim may already be nearly perfect. With a ring sight (no pin inside the ring), your aiming is less perfect because you have no pin to set in the middle of the middle of the target. You only have a ring to set the gold inside of. This allows you to think less of the criticalness of aiming and shoot a much smoother and more perfect arrow.

What's a handy rule for correcting a bowsight setting?

Move the sight in the direction the arrows are striking the target, not in the direction you want them to move. For instance, if your arrow is high left, your arrow rest must go down and right. When you move your sight to the position of the bad arrow, it in effect is pushing the arrow rest to a corrected position.

If I'm shooting a 12-strand string, what would be the effects of a 10-strand string and 14-strand string on that same bow?

The 10-strand string would be lighter, consequently you would get a slightly faster arrow. But it would also react faster and would be more critical to any mistakes the archer made. It is a less strong string and will not last as long. A 14-strand string is heavier, producing a slower arrow and less critical performance. The string will, to a slight degree, absorb and smooth out some minor mistake you may make in release. It will also be a stronger string.

In which direction should I twist a string for fine tuning?

Always twist in the *same direction* the serving is wound around the string, so the serving is constantly tightening. Obviously, if you need to lengthen the string slightly, you will need to unwind it slightly; but never go back beyond the original twist of the string. If you see that you are about to do this, you need a longer string than the one you're now using.

Why twist a string at all?

A string should have 6-10 twists in it at all times. The twists will make the string rounder, and any flat spot will cause the string to plane against the air. A string can be twisted too much; the strings fit more closely together and create more friction, which causes a breakage of an inside strand. *A string with even only one broken strand is unsafe, and must be replaced immediately.*

Why "shoot in" a spare string?

A string will change slightly in the first 20-30 arrows shot from it. It is stretching slightly and the strands are settling in. After this point, the string will shoot uniformly. Since all strings are slightly different, if you break a string in the middle of competition, you should know exactly where the spare string shoots. *Never go to a tournament unprepared.*

What are the differences between monofilament and nylon serving?

Monofilament provides for a slightly cleaner release and tends to last longer without fraying. But if mono breaks, it will unwind totally (unless it is glued). With nylon, you have a chance to save it and tie it off properly before it can unwind.

How tightly should the nock fit on the string?

Just tight enough to hold the arrow on the string itself. If you bounce the string with your finger, the arrow should be able to fall off.

What is an easy, quick test for arrow straightness and nock alignment?

Roll the arrow across a table top or a piece of glass. Spin it over the V of your thumbnail and tip of index finger. It will wobble if it is crooked.

How will arrows for indoor versus outdoor use differ?

You need a faster arrow outdoors to get through the wind and reach the long distances. Indoors, you should have a slightly heavier, less critical, more forgiving arrow to help you maintain pinpoint accuracy.

If a person wants to shoot outdoors and indoors, but can afford only one bow, what guidelines should he use?

This depends on whether you will be shooting FITA or field outdoors. The longest field archery shot is 80 yards, while the longest FITA target is just about 100 yards. Field archery is generally more closed in by trees and brush, so wind will be less of a factor than in FITA shooting. As a result, you may need a slightly faster bow for FITA shooting. Either way, get the best bow you can afford. You might consider a takedown bow, with a stronger set of limbs for outdoor shooting and a less heavy set of limbs for indoor shooting.

How do heat/humidity affect bow performance and arrow flight?

A humid day will cause the loss of a yard or so because the air is heavier and creates more friction on the arrow as it flies. Higher elevation with less dense air will add distance capabilities to the bow and arrow. And you will generally tire more quickly under these conditions, especially if you are not conditioned for them.

How do shooting into and with the wind affect arrow flight?

With the wind you should aim lower because you will gain yardage capabilities. Into the wind you should aim slightly higher because the wind is a resistant force.

On what do you focus the eye when aiming?

Focus on the target and let the sight become blurred. The sight is close enough to the eye to allow critical enough aiming even if it is slightly fuzzy. Remember, you are aiming at the target; if it is in focus, your mind will also be concentrating on it.

What type of arrow rest is best for target shooting?

One of the finger-type rests of plastic or metal. This type will provide solid support and not create drag on the arrow. It will also be slightly forgiving.

What is a pressure button and what does it do?

It is a spring-loaded metal plunger fitted horizontally through the riser so the plunger emerges at the point the arrow lies on the arrow rest. It absorbs some of the side pressure given to the arrow upon the shot and helps the arrow straighten out faster into smooth flight. It thus can help provide better arrow flight to an arrow that may not be ideally matched to the bow and your release.

What do I do when I have made a bad shot?

Make the corrections in your head and equipment, then forget it. Relax and then begin your proper positive concentration on the next shot.

What's the best thing to do for a blister?

Break it. If you develop a blister under a callus, you are going to lose the callus unless you break the blister and keep it drained and dry.   It will also heal faster.

How does a person cure freezing, target panic, and creeping?

All three are mentally based problems that manifest themselves as breakdowns in form, especially creeping, which is directly related to a loss of back tension. Freezing is an early stage of target panic wherein you cannot bring the sight onto the bull's-eye. In target panic, your form sort of explodes as you try to anticipate release when struggling to bring the sight onto the bull's-eye; you often swing the sight across the bull's-eye and release as you swing.

You can correct them by conquering your mental approach, or by adding a clicker. In the mental correction, try going back to the empty target and shooting a lighter bow with your eyes closed. This will allow you to groove your form positively.

When does the first slump hit, and how does a person work out of it?

Slumps are relative. You can hit one a month or two after you begin archery, or not until nine or ten months have passed, or maybe not at all. But it is relative to how well you are shooting before the slump. A good shooter might define a leveling off in scores as a slump. A mediocre shooter might define a decrease in scores as a slump.

Many conditions create a slump: form breakdown, inconsistent practice, too much practice. So your efforts to work out of a slump will depend on the reason for the slump. If your form has suffered, go back to basic form practice. If you have practiced inconsistently, try to set up a better practice routine. If you have graded yourself 50/50 on form and score, grade yourself 75/25 with the higher emphasis on form. If you have practiced so much that shooting has become monotonous, shoot an entirely different type of archery or shoot some archery games or stop shooting entirely for a while. The change in routine will refresh you and make you eager, after a while, to get back into the groove.

chapter eight

mental attitude

There's almost no way to describe the intense personal satisfaction of knowing you've shot a good arrow. You've built your form and tuned your equipment and now you've put it all together. You know the instant the arrow leaves the bow whether it will be good or not; and if it is good, you have that fleeting moment of satisfaction to mark it in your mind as an individual triumph of positive thinking and good preparation.

And then you must forget it and do it over again, and again, and again, just as well each time.

But there's a long distance between the consistent good arrow after arrow and that time long ago—or so it often seems—when you first discovered archery and its potential rewards. There will be mental peaks and valleys, times of satisfaction and frustration, of anger and determination. But you have persevered through it all.

Why? How?

To some people archery will always be a kind of pageantry, to others simply a beautiful sport or perhaps a projection of themselves. To some people, who never hunt, it's a way to compete or enjoy a family sport. To some, who never compete but enjoy the outdoors and like to hunt, it's a way to combine both activities. To someone in a wheelchair, it's an activity in which to compete on an equal basis with anyone. To a young boy or girl it's something to do to impress family and friends. It's a way to excel in competition, or a way to relax. Archery leads to travel, meeting people, enjoying a unique shared experience. It is a test of self and an expression of self.

Which leads into the "how" of archery's mental approach.

I strongly believe that you compete only against yourself. If you know yourself, and know what you can do, then there is no way you can beat yourself.

The reason you sometimes see archers frantically looking for some new shooting style or piece of equipment to solve their problem is that at one time or another they shot well. Now they aren't shooting that well, so they feel something is drastically wrong. In truth, there may not be anything wrong. No shooter remains the same year after year. Strength, mental attitude, time available to practice, laziness, or whatever . . . they all contribute to ups and downs.

To some people, shooting well is the total fulfillment. Without that, they have nothing. But for any competitor it's hard to go to an archery tournament, shoot badly, and maintain a good mood. Most archers cannot talk "winning or losing," but they can talk "placing." For instance, just before and at the Olympics in 1972, I was shooting FITA scores in the 1240s and 1250s. That's tailed off to around 1200 most of the time because I'm not shooting as much, and not shooting the FITA Round as much. So now, when I shoot a 1200 or just over that, I have to be happy with it. I couldn't truthfully expect any better, even though I know I can shoot better and have shot better.

You must always judge yourself on the immediate past, not the distant past. In the distant past, you were probably a different shooter.

This is why you must have the proper positive mental approach. In a tournament, for instance, the "distant past" can be one or two arrows ago. The good shot feels good right at the moment; then you lose much of that euphoria as the shot fades away among other shots you've made. If you shoot a bad arrow, its memory should fade the same way. This doesn't always happen, and leads to a negative approach. For some people the effects of a bad shot will hold over for the next few arrows. For others, it will hold over for days.

But each arrow is an individual, and should be treated as such. If you shoot a good arrow and it feels good, beautiful. If you shoot a bad arrow and it feels terrible, OK, you still have other arrows. So shoot them, and shoot them well.

Let's start the development of a good mental attitude right at the beginning—when you're just practicing for practice's sake, with no tournament in the immediate future. You're just going out to strengthen your form and keep your muscles in tone. I try to do one of two things: (1) shoot strictly for form, at a very close distance, usually indoors, or (2) shoot the most difficult distance possible, usually the 90-meter FITA distance. I believe this would be a valid practice approach for most archers.

The purpose of this is that, for a tournament, you have some specific goals you want to shoot; but these may not be the goals of another archer. Thus, as you practice, you don't have to beat anyone else; you just need to beat yourself.

To maintain a positive attitude, you need to first shoot a given amount of time each day strictly for form, and shoot a given amount of time each day for score *and* form. When you are shooting for score, to keep this positive mental attitude, set goals for yourself that are easily achievable. Do this all the time, not just when you first begin. I still do this, and it works.

For instance, if a FITA shooter shoots 280 at 90 meters, which is a good score, he could set a minimum practice goal of 240 or thereabout. When he shoots anything above that, he feels good. The 240 is not so much a goal as it is a low minimum. You obviously cannot set any maximum, because that would be a perfect score.

I believe setting a minimum, under which you will not allow yourself to slide, will help maintain the proper attitude much better than setting a goal that you may attain only sporadically. Because if you get a bad day, you're going to break your back reaching for that goal. On a good day, you'd have no trouble reaching it.

For instance, if you have a goal of 245 (at 90 meters on the FITA Round), and you shoot a 242, you're three points under. And you're three points under right up there in your head. But if your minimum goal had been 240, you would be two points over, and you would be well on the way to building a positive mental attitude.

Remember, you're shooting partly for score, partly for form. And all the time during form and score work, you're working on your head. You are getting smoothed out when shooting for form, and hopefully shooting better than minimum when shooting for score.

Score is thus a method of test and reward, to find out how well you've done on form development. I've always found that I can't *just* shoot arrows. When my form needs work, I can practice for form alone. But if my form is quite well set, I can't go out and practice just to shoot arrows. I don't believe anyone else can, either. You and I might start out shooting arrows in nice, tight groups, but by the time we finished we would be using the entire matt. There would be no goal—not even a minimum goal—and no directive. In effect, we would be tearing down, not building.

Remember, if Joe sets a goal of 240 and Pete sets a goal of 245—yet they both shoot 243—Joe will eventually beat Pete because he (Joe) is three points up in his head and Pete is two points down.

Some archers like to shoot to beat someone else, instead of shooting to beat their goal. But right away they have put themselves in second place and placed themselves under pressure. If they react well to this type of pressure, fine. However, if the person they are shooting to beat doesn't falter, but reaches his own personal goal, the second shooter doesn't stand a chance. A lot depends on how that second shooter responds to various types of pressure, but I believe that person is at a disadvantage psychologically.

If you can beat yourself—match or better your goal—you have no right to complain. If you beat yourself, and you don't win the tournament, there's no doubt that the person who beat you shot better than you did. You can't do anything about that, but you have come away with a strong positive attitude that will help you in future tournaments.

The only possible exception I can see is in the FITA Round, or a similar scoring round, which has the 10-ring and 9-ring in the gold. If your groups tighten up enough, and the top person's groups don't, then you can catch up sometimes.

It's doubtful that you should move up the minimum goals from one year to the next, unless you're improving so drastically that you are in effect a different archer from the one you were last year. Yet, you have no assurance that you will continue to maintain this level of performance, so you may be jeopardizing your proper positive mental attitude if you boost your minimum goal.

You must set reasonably attainable goals. Tell yourself "I want more than 40 points each end at 90 meters." After that, if weather permits and you are shooting well, tell yourself "I'm going to be happy above 40, but I'd like to shoot a 270 total (45 points per end). Right away, you've got a five-point jump each end. You're bound to reach one of these goals. If you make the 270, great; you've mastered two minimum goals that day. If you don't make the 270, you still reached 50 percent of your goals. You won't be too happy about missing the 270, but on the other hand you didn't shoot too badly, either. If you had, you would not have reached that 40-points-per-end goal.

Now it's a month before a specific tournament. You begin honing things in your head. Now you see a chance for your work to pay off. There's a possibility you may shoot well, even win. You concentrate a little more. Nothing really changes much; the conditions are just magnified. You will shoot more arrows for score, more arrows for form.

If you shoot twice as many arrows per day as you will in the tournament, you know you're in physical shape. In shooting that much, and in knowing you're in that good a physical condition, your mental condition will improve, too. You know you won't get tired. You know your fingers won't get sore. You have shot your equipment so much that it isn't equipment any more; it's you. It all blends together into a haze, with a fine line of distinction between the equipment and you.

With everything going right, you begin to feel yourself peaking. This is a near perfect physical and mental attitude or condition. Physically, you can shoot well; mentally, you know you can shoot well. The combination of the two almost undoubtedly causes you to shoot well. Unless, of course, something destroys one of the two, and then you're off your peak anyway.

It's always nice to peak the *day before* a tournament. Not a week before, but the day before. You can tell. You go out to the shooting line to practice the night before the tournament. It's about 6-7 P.M., you've met a lot of old friends, you've joshed and laughed, met a few new people. You're back in a familiar element that you know and like.

Say you want to shoot a 270 at 90 meters. You start shooting, and the 50s, 51s, 52s, and 53s on practice ends start coming. You know, right then, that you're on. It places you in such a good mental attitude that nothing the next day will keep you from shooting well. The only problem could be that if you do get a bit nervous, and don't shoot well the first end, you have a more difficult time keeping the good mental attitude. (Again, the person who likes to come in as the underdog might do well under this particular circumstance.)

New shooters, of course, won't have the familiarity of place and peers. The first-time shooter will probably hope to shoot as well as he did at home. But this is just like the conditions all rookies in all sports meet. He should relax, rely on his form, try to match or beat his personal goals. If he does that, he's on the road.

Zero hour? This is strictly an individual thing, governed by how you react to pressure. It's also an individual thing as to how much pressure you'll let yourself be placed under. I believe this may be the key—the resistance to external stimuli and the dependency on what *you* know of yourself.

For instance, before I was 15 I didn't know what pressure was. I had never been extremely close to another shooter in score; I was always either way above or way below. I just went to the tournament and shot my arrows. I was just a dumb little kid. But now that I've been in some good competition, pushing and getting pushed, I get butterflies. This is only natural. And I think it's good. If a person, in any sport, ever reaches a point where he does not get butterflies just before competition begins, that person is in the wrong sport.

In archery, this is why it is good to shoot against yourself as long as you are realistic with your goals and not just plain lazy. You are not letting anyone else interfere, or put pressure on you in any way. When you reach actual competition, no one can put pressure on you, whether that person is ahead, behind, or tied. And you're certainly not going to worry about that other shooter. You will always maintain some semblance of a positive mental attitude.

If something goes wrong with your form, something has gone wrong upstairs. Your brain controls your body. If you fall downstairs and bruise a couple of muscles, your body obviously might not want to do what the brain wants it to do. But if all conditions are favorable, if you maintain good positive attitude, your form will be there. At this stage, it should be natural to you. You know what to do, you know when you want to do it, and you know how to do it. So if the body doesn't do it, your head isn't in control.

Subconscious? On the tournament line, I'll try most of the time to let my subconscious take over. I believe most shooters do the same. The form has become natural, with everything trained and ready to do what it is supposed to do. The mind has gone through this thousands upon thousands of times. It knows what a good shot feels like and it knows how to get there.

There definitely is a physical memory, too. If you stop shooting for two weeks, you had better have six weeks to prepare. The first day you come back, you will probably shoot a good score. You will probably do the same on the second day. But heaven forbid the third day! The muscles have retained some of what they knew, but they have relaxed, become lazier. And when you come back, you shoot fewer arrows the first couple of days. Your muscles can withstand this. So you push harder. But all of a sudden things aren't working like you intended. You have lost the strength and muscle tone to really dig into a long, constructive practice. Now you must build them back up.

Your brain is not going to forget, but neither will it be as sharp. The commands from brain to muscle will be slower. The first few days you were relaxed, more or less reacquainting yourself with an old, familiar routine. So you shot well. Then when you intensified the effort, the tuned reserve wasn't there, and this is why you intensify efforts as you near tournament time.

Shooters often wonder why a person gets "hot" at a specific tournament. I believe this is because that particular archer goes into a state where his subconscious is more conscious than his conscious. The subconscious mind can control the body so much more than can the conscious mind.

The conscious mind has so many more things going on—someone

kicks a chair and the conscious mind knows it. Someone breaks a bowstring right beside you while you are at full draw. The conscious mind
knows this happened, and is shocked. But the subconscious mind
seems to be able to use the conscious mind as a buffer zone, allowing
stimuli to filter through slowly. Nor do stimuli get through with the
same shock, and they are not treated the same. You will know the
bowstring broke; but you won't react. The subconscious mind *knows* it
won't affect you, but the conscious mind *thinks it may*.

Concentration benefits the subconscious rather than the conscious,
and helps the subconscious come to the surface more easily. This is
why it becomes easier to shoot in tournaments as you gain tournament
experience. You get on the line, yet you don't know that someone is
standing next to you. There's you, the target, the bow, and the arrow.
The bow and the arrow are actually you, to a degree. The target is
something projected out there a short distance to be reckoned with.

The arrow in the target is the logical culmination of the shot. It is the
reward or the punishment. If it becomes a reward, it feeds upon itself
back to you and improves your confidence and attitude. If it tells you
how you shot a bad arrow, you must make the correction—mentally
and/or physically, depending on the error—and then forget the
negative.

If you have practiced enough, you will nearly always know before
the arrow reaches the target whether it is good or bad. And if it is bad,
you will generally be able to tell where it will hit, and why.

Some archers say they can get outside themselves and watch themselves shoot. I get more inside myself. It's not that I watch myself, in
a sense, but that I can feel myself. I've watched myself enough times
on tape that I know when a shot feels a certain way it will look that
same way.

There's one more element to positive mental attitude—fun, the
simple joy of doing something you like, such as shooting a bow and
arrow accurately.

It is a joyful fun when you shoot well, and a positively oriented determination when you shoot less than well. If you win a tournament,
you could probably run a marathon right afterward; if you shoot
poorly, it will be a physical and mental struggle just to drive home.

The mental aspect works much harder when you are shooting below expectations. And when you are going right, you are not wasting movement or thought process. You are conserving energy, and even building up a reserve. You get stronger. Like a machine, the fewer moving parts you employ, the less can go wrong.

Archery still will be fun, even when it is aggravating. Archery is easy to learn, but difficult to master. Yet there is always the possibility of a reward, no matter how poorly you shot, or thought you shot. You go to the next tournament and hope you will shoot better. Each time there is the reward potential—either of being in twenty-second place and shooting the best score you ever shot, or of winning it all.

This relates to the pleasures and rewards of shooting against yourself. If you shoot the best ever, you will be pleased no matter where you placed. You will enjoy the people, the travel, the shooting, the memories of long hours of agonizing practice, the potential of even more rewards.

Sportsmanship is a basic element, too; sportsmanship combined with common sense. The basic thing is to be gracious in everything you do, no matter how you're shooting. If you're shooting poorly, there's no reason to take out your frustration on the person standing next to you on the line by losing control of yourself or bothering him in some other way. That person has no bearing on how well or how poorly you shoot. Again, this comes back to the earlier credo —"Shoot only against yourself."

Part of the reason you're at an archery tournament is to make friends. So go ahead and be friendly, if that is good. Don't be so outgoing that you forget to shoot an end; this has happened, much to the shooter's chagrin. No matter how good or bad you shoot, you're here because you enjoy the sport. And the people you meet on the way up will most likely be the people you'll meet on the way down.

You also have certain responsibilities to the tournament as a whole and to the other people shooting on the target with you. Offer to keep score, especially if you want to; and even if you don't want to. If certain duties at the target are assigned, do your duty willingly and accurately. If the duties are not assigned, select the various duties democratically or toss a coin.

On the line, keep basically to yourself. Don't try to affect other shooters. There's no reason to show temper; this only hurts you and helps someone else. If another shooter is watching you, that shooter judges your show of temper as a sign that you are dissatisfied with your shooting. That shooter knows you are shooting poorly and immediately knows you are one less person to be concerned about. This reinforces that person's positive attitude, not yours.

In the process of attending and shooting at tournaments, archery will teach you a lot about yourself. You will learn your true desires —how strongly you want to achieve, how you handle the frustration of slumps, how you work your way out of them, how you respond to internal and external pressure, how to pace yourself for maximum results over long periods of time, how to maintain your enthusiasm. Do this to your own satisfaction and you will develop considerable self-confidence, the kind of confidence that will make you a more complete archer and a more complete person. Archery may be your whole life, or it may only be a part of it. Either way, it will be a benefit.

chapter nine

archery safety

Archery is safe; some *archers* are not safe. To make archery the fully enjoyable sport it should be, you must be aware of unsafe archers, unsafe equipment, and unsafe practices. A strung bow is powerful even when not drawn; a string or limb can break and pieces will fly anywhere.

So use common sense and courtesy when you are handling archery tackle, on and off the shooting line. The basic safety guidelines given here are standard everywhere. If you have additional local safety conditions, be sure you are fully aware of them.

GENERAL SAFETY

- Don't take a chance. Goofing around and horseplay have no place in archery. Inventive games, such as tin cans thrown in the air, are not appropriate on an ordinary target line.

- In organized shoots, and practice, don't shoot at anything not on targets on the target range.

- Respect the power of the bow—at brace height and when fully drawn with arrow nocked.
- Be properly supervised if you're just beginning to learn archery.
- Don't shoot arrows straight up to see how high they will go; they tend to come straight back down.
- Don't point a nocked arrow anywhere but at the target.
- Don't take chances.

CLOTHING

- Wear comfortable shoes, to protect your feet should you inadvertently step on an arrow when searching for it, and to be able to stand on the shooting line for several hours without developing sore feet.
- Shirts and blouses should have short sleeves, no pockets on bow side, form-fitting body (preferably a tight T-shirt or knit nylon top).
- Tie long hair back securely, and keep it back of your shoulders.
- Chest protectors are not required, but many archers prefer to use them.
- Contact lenses for beginners are a "no-no" because the first few arrows are so jarring that the lenses may pop out. Glasses are more difficult to shoot with, but must be endured until the archer reaches higher skill.

EQUIPMENT

- Check equipment every time before you begin shooting. Be sure the string is properly seated in string notches and groove of a recurve, firm attachments on takedown bows, arrows are of proper length, hand or finger sling is firm and unworn. Check for these possible problems: cracked nocks, loose servings, frayed bowstring (basically around loop ends, which can give way suddenly), bent or cracked arrows, twisted bow limbs, parted or cracked laminations in limbs or handle, loose arrow rest, mis-set sight (causing you to miss target on first shot), loose nocking locator on string. On compound bows, also check S-hooks to be sure they're not bent out, check eccentric wheels for cracks, idler assemblies for tightness, cable for wear, all screws and bolts for tightness.

CARE

- Don't store bows upright. Hang them by the string, or lay them flat on a rack with two supports close to handle riser.
- Don't store equipment in dry heat.
- Have a heavy enough case so equipment will not be damaged.
- Waxing bow strings ensures longer string life.
- Wipe off wet bows, especially the limbs, and the moving parts of compound bows.
- Never release a string without an arrow on it. Doing so could damage the limbs. If you practice drawing and anchoring without an arrow, let the bow down slowly.

ON THE RANGE

- Have adequate distance behind targets. Outdoors, this should be 30-50 yards, and should be roped off. Indoors, the arrows must not be able to glance off the backstop, but either penetrate or be absorbed.
- Have adequate distance behind the shooting line for the seating of competitors and hanging of equipment.
- The only people allowed on the shooting line are shooters.
- Have adequate distance to sides of target.
- When one person walks to a target, everyone walks.
- Only nock an arrow when it is pointing toward the target. Be think-

ing only of shooting. If you are interrupted, un-nock the arrow and place it back in the quiver.

- If at all possible, have adequate bow rack facilities. This saves leaning the bow against an arrow, or laying it on the ground.

- Place the bow in front of the target when looking for arrows behind it. This tells other archers that it's not safe to shoot.

- Always wear armguard and finger tab. If you don't, a sore arm and sore fingers can spoil your form.

- Be sure no one is at or behind the target when you begin shooting.

- Always use a quiver of some sort. Not only is it easier to carry the arrows, but the fletching will be better protected than if you were to carry them in your hand. You will also be in less danger of inadvertently jabbing someone with nock or point.

- Pull arrows backward from grass, gently lifting the nock and fletching, if the fletching has *not* penetrated into the grass. If it has, gently lift the tip of the arrow and slide the arrow forward and out. This will not harm the fletching.

- Pull arrows *straight* out of the target. Place one hand against the target around the arrow and pull the arrow with the other hand. If the arrow sticks, twist it slightly until it loosens. If the point is in wood, grasp the arrow close to the tip and wiggle it loose. If fletching is buried in the target, pull the arrow through, forward.

- Don't crowd against other archers on the shooting line.

- Obey the field captain's whistle blasts, one to start shooting and two to stop shooting.

- Do not stand directly behind a person pulling arrows.

FIELD ARCHERY

- No more than two spectators per target, standing behind the shooters but moving with them from target to target.

- The range should be cleared sufficiently to allow light bows to be shot, allowing at least a 15-foot path.

- Never shoot toward a target other than your own.
- Shoot broadheads only where signs and conditions permit. If the range is not posted, don't shoot them.
- Shoot only from designated field stakes. Don't free-lance your shooting position.
- It is especially important here to leave your bow in front of the target when searching for arrows because you may be obscured in underbrush behind the target.
- On elevated shots, check the security of the steps, especially in wet weather.

BOWHUNTING

- Use a bow stringer; it is more secure and will not twist limbs. And it makes stringing heavy bows much easier.
- Don't lean on the tip of a strung bow. It can unstring with disastrous results.
- Never draw another person's bow without permission. Never overdraw a short bow. This can lead to breakage.
- Have arrows that match your draw length or are just slightly longer. Arrows that are too short allow overdrawing and possible cutting of your bow hand fingers. Arrows too long decrease speed and accuracy.
- Don't run with an arrow on the bow. Don't cross fences with an arrow on the bow. Don't have an arrow on the bow in camp or when not hunting.
- Be sure of your target. Never point an arrow at anything you don't intend to shoot.
- Always be especially cautious handling broadheads. A slip can cut you or the bowstring, hurting the bow and you.
- Always carry broadheads in a quiver with protection over the heads, should you fall or stumble.
- Be careful stalking game in heavily hunted areas; if you are prop-

erly camouflaged and moving right you will be hard to see and may sound like a deer.

- Be careful when climbing trees. Bark is slippery in mornings and during rain or snow.
- Use a rope to lift bow, arrows, and other gear into and down from tree stands. Do not carry tackle in your hand or on your back while climbing.
- Tie a safety rope around yourself when in a tree stand, should you fall asleep.
- Approach wounded game cautiously.
- Mark the trail when tracking game so you don't get lost.
- Be familiar with the area you will hunt. Carry maps, a compass, matches. Know how to use the safety gear.
- Carry a small first-aid kit with bandages, compress, and tourniquet.
- Be sure you are in good enough physical condition for plenty of walking, climbing, and, hopefully, transporting game.
- Should you become lost, do not panic. Sit down, rest, and calm yourself. Then get to high ground, or climb a tree, to note landmarks to use as direction aids.

chapter ten

muscles and exercises

The accurate shooting of an arrow demands precision and positive control in your physical movements. You need physical tone and physical strength, and you must know how to apply them properly to the shot. In target archery, you must reproduce as identically as possible, for shot after shot, the individual movements in the total shot sequence. Knowing that you have the strength and muscle tone to do this will aid your coordination and your confidence, which will then help you avoid many of the common tournament tensions.

In bowhunting, you must have the strength to shoot *accurately* as heavy a bow as you can handle, and you must have the skill and control to do this properly on the first shot.

Your mastery of the muscles involved in an archery shot is complicated by the fact that some muscles are used statically, while others are used dynamically. However, with practice you can blend these various muscle movements into one of the most beautiful physical actions to be seen—the positive, controlled, accurate shooting of an arrow. When you have made that good shot—knowing exactly how you did it—your pleasure and confidence will increase immeasurably.

When working to build *strength and tone,* do not try to develop bulk. Large, bulky muscles, though powerful, may not have the suppleness required to withstand the constant stretching and contracting needed for shot after shot. The bulkily muscled person will also have more troubles with string clearance then will a slimmer person.

Above all, building muscle strength and tone should not be drudgery. Exercising may not exactly be the highlight of your day, so you should try to make it as enjoyable as possible. Doing so will ease the mental approach, as well as the physical approach.

I like to run, so I run quite a bit. I don't lift weights because I don't like to lift weights. But I *do* shoot a heavy bow with considerable repetition, and this helps build strength. If you don't like to run, just jog around the block three times a week. This will exercise your heart and structural muscles, increasing blood flow and stamina. Or skip rope for a few minutes each day. Do a few pushups each day. If this is difficult at first, do them from your knees. Or place your feet three feet from a wall and push back from the wall. Or sit in a strong chair and lift yourself from it, pushing down on the sides of the chair seat or the arms.

To build strength in your hands and fingers, straighten and tense the fingers of one hand and push the tips up against the resisting pressure of your other hand. Squeeze a rubber ball a few times each day. Or, for maximum power building, do finger pushups. To add flexibility to your fingers, so you can come off the bowstring more cleanly, push back against each finger, singly or as a group, stretching the muscles against their natural movement.

To build shoulder and back muscles, lean against a wall and push your body away with both elbows. Or hook the fingers of both hands together and try to pull them apart. Then place both palms together and try to push them through each other. Place both hands under a heavy table and try to lift it, while you are seated. Or stand in a doorway and try to push the door frame apart. (If you're already super-strong, have a carpenter handy.) Or draw and let down several times a bow that is heavier than the one you are now shooting.

Most of these simple exercises can be done in idle moments at home, on the way to work, at work, when you are watching television or listening to music.

Many of these exercises are isometric. They should be balanced with isotonic exercises. You must remain supple and flexible. You do not want to become musclebound. Leave the bulges to the beach crowd.

Swimming is a good all-around exercise. It strengthens inner and outer muscles. It aids breathing and heartbeat. And it is a *change*. You cannot shoot archery all the time and remain sharp. Darned few people thrive on monotony; no one should be expected to. You may think you thrive on archery, but even a zealot must take a break now and then. The change will add perspective to your total life, and to your archery. It will also help you stay enthusiastic. Following a change in routine, no matter how short, you will be eager to return to archery. And you will do better because of this positive approach. Most archers enjoy other sports, too. Don't neglect your other enjoyments, but channel them as you wish.

WHICH MUSCLES ARE USED?

Most of the muscles used in archery are, obviously, in the arms and back. But leg, hip, and body trunk muscles also come into play. The flexors and extensors on the drawing arm side of your body will be needed to help hold your body standing with the correct alignment and rigidity, while the same muscles on the bow arm side of your body will help balance this control but won't provide as much of the strength for power control. The abductors (movement away from vertical midline of your body) in your pelvic region will help control proper turning at the hips, and will also help control your stance no matter how far apart or close together your feet are placed.

The sternomastoid muscle on the drawing arm side of your neck, the muscles on the bow arm side of your upper spinal region, and some of the upper trapezius muscles all rotate your neck and help you hold a strong, but relaxed, head attitude. They also help raise the sternum for better breathing and breath control.

When you raise your bow and hold it in position, the deltoids raise the arm, with additional help from the supraspinatus muscles. Most of the work is done by the middle and posterior sections of the deltoid.

The pronator teres muscle rotates your elbow out of the string path.

174

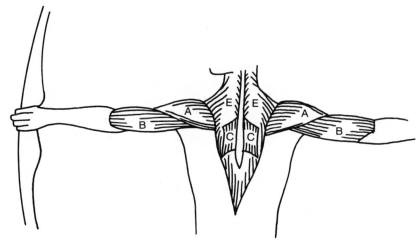

Back view of upper body muscles: A, deltoids; B, triceps;
C, rhomboids; E, trapezius

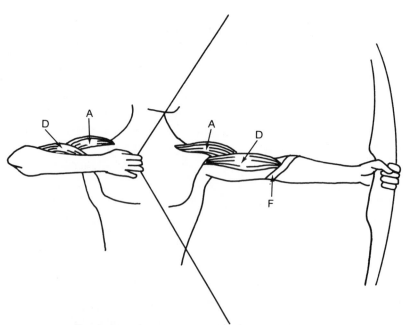

Front view of upper body muscles: A, deltoids; D, biceps;
F, pronator teres

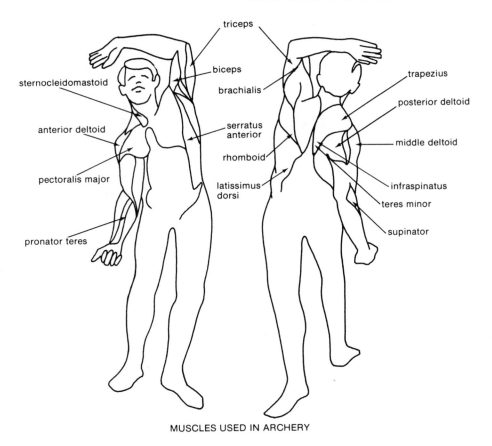

sternocleidomastoid

triceps

biceps

brachialis

anterior deltoid

serratus
anterior

rhomboid

pectoralis major

latissimus
dorsi

pronator teres

trapezius

posterior deltoid

middle deltoid

infraspinatus

teres minor

supinator

MUSCLES USED IN ARCHERY

This is called "pronation of the forearm, or elbow."

Flexor (increase the angle) and tensor (decrease the angle) muscles on the two sides of your bow forearm hold your wrist firmly in a static contraction to resist pressure of the bow.

Triceps keep your bow arm extended. Biceps on the bow arm are relatively relaxed.

As you draw, other muscles exert their influence. The drawing arm bicep contracts your arm into the proper angle as the rhomboids (probably the most important muscles in the draw-aim-release sequence) and middle trapezius muscles draw your shoulder blades (scapulae) together. The lower part of the trapezius keeps your shoulders from hunching up. Your bow arm shoulder blade is rotated upward and adducted (moved toward the spine) as the pressure on your draw increases, and since there is a tendency for the shoulder girdle to rotate, minor pectoral and subclavian (under the collar bone) muscles hold your bow arm shoulder down.

Even though your bow arm shoulder blade tends to move, it does not move as much as your drawing arm shoulder blade. Continued back tension is assisted mainly by the posterior deltoid, infraspinatus, and teres minor muscles, with some help from the latissimus dorsi.

To release the string, you continue the above-mentioned back tension and relax the flexor muscles in your fingers.

Your drawing arm muscles are in phasic (moving, dynamic) contraction and your bow arm muscles are in static contraction.

EXERCISES

To develop your muscles properly so you can control the bow you shoot, you must force your muscles into an overload training program.

This can be done, in part, by the isometric exercises mentioned earlier. If you employ any exercises that closely duplicate actual movements you make during the shooting of an arrow, try to duplicate exactly the shooting positions as you apply maximum effort. Do each isometric exercise once a day, and hold it for six seconds.

You should begin any physical training program before you begin your archery season, if your shooting is not year-round. This will give you the opportunity to reach a higher level of physical tone and strength when you begin the serious preparation for competitive shooting or hunting.

The cardiorespiratory (heart/lungs) programs increase the efficiency of the heart to force more blood throughout the body, causing the lungs to exchange more oxygen for waste materials, bringing more energy and carrying away residue lactic acid (which causes soreness and fatigue). Increased blood circulation also helps distribute the right amount of lactic acid in the muscles, for a certain amount is definitely needed.

It has been estimated that it takes at least six weeks of relaxed, smooth running with alternating periods of rest, or walking, to develop a high level of cardiorespiratory fitness, and about two months of isotonic exercises before good gains are made. Once you are in good shape, you should run or jog one day, lift weights the next. This will keep you fit and loose.

The following isotonic exercises will increase body strength. Use relatively light weights and do several repetitions. This will build strength, but will hold down bulk.

Muscle	Exercise
Forearm	
flexors	squeeze rubber ball, roll up weight tied to a stick (palms down), wrist curls with palms up
extensors	wrist curls with palms down
Upper arm	
biceps	chin-ups with fingers toward the body, curls with barbells (palms up)
triceps	push-ups, dips on parallel bars, presses with barbells, dumbbell press
Shoulder and back	
deltoid	pull springs apart in front of chest, lateral raises with dumbbells, press barbells, upright row, press with dumbbells
latissimus dorsi	wide arm chin-ups (behind the neck)

teres major	bent-over row, straight arm pullover in prone position
trapezius	shoulder shrugs, pull springs apart in front of chest
rhomboids	wide arm chin-ups (behind the neck), pull springs apart, with wall weights face wall with arms horizontal and pull arms down to side

LATERAL RAISE, STANDING
Bend at shoulders only

LATERAL RAISE, LEANING
Bend at shoulders only

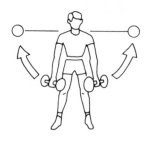

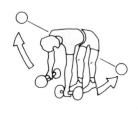

TWO ARM CURL
Bend arms at elbows, lift toward shoulders. Can be done with bar-bell or dumbbells

SHOULDER SHRUG
Lift shoulders and shoulder blades up and in

PRESS
Lying on back, lift barbell straight up from chest. If you are standing, lift weight overhead

STRAIGHT-ARM PULLOVER
Lie on back, arms extended overhead. Lift weight up and over to waist. Arms remain straight

WRIST CURL
With arms slightly flexed, lift barbell or dumbbells with wrist movement only. You may wish to let weight roll slightly toward fingertips

BENT-OVER ROW
Pull barbell or dumbbells up toward chest. You may wish to pull weight up to belt buckle, then forward to about shoulders, then down

glossary

AAC: American Archery Council.

Address: Assuming proper stance in preparation to shoot an arrow.

Adjustable pressure point: Spring-loaded plunger fitted horizontally through bow at exact point arrow lies on arrow rest. Absorbs some of the side pressure placed on the arrow at the moment of release and thus helps arrow to stabilize earlier in flight.

Alignment: Relationship of eye-string-sight and target center at full draw.

AMO: Archery Manufacturers Organization.

Anchor point: A specific location on the face or under the jawbone, with which the index finger (and sometimes the thumb) of the drawing hand makes contact at full draw for consistent shooting.

Archer's paradox: Cycles of bending left and right the arrow undergoes as it leaves the bow, gradually stabilizing into smooth flight. Created by impetus of string force on the arrow.

Archery golf: Game played with bow and usually special arrows on a golf course, or a specially designed course for archery golf, using golf scoring system.

Armguard: Leather or plastic device worn on the inside of the bow forearm to protect from string sting.

Arrow plate: A piece of leather above the arrow rest glued to bow window. It provides horizontal point contact on the arrow.

Arrow rest: A projection on the cutout side of the bow window on which the arrow rests. Made of plastic, wire, bristles, animal hair, carpet-like material.

Back: The part of the bow away from the archer.

Backed bow: Bow made with a protection of rawhide or fiberglass on the back.

Balloon feather: A parabolic cut feather.

Barb: A projection on a fishing or hunting arrowhead that prevents easy withdrawal.

Blunt: An arrow tip that is flat, used for small game hunting.

Bolt: The crossbow equivalent of an arrow, usually 14''-16'' long.

Bounce out: Arrow strikes target and rebounds back toward archer.

Bow arm: Arm that lifts and holds the bow during a shot.

Bow sight: A mechanical device attached to the bow, which helps the archer aim at the target.

Bow sling: A leather strap attached to the bow that allows the archer's hand to remain in contact with the bow without gripping it.

Bow stave: Piece of wood from which a bow is made.

Bowstring: The string of a bow, usually made of Dacron.

Bow-tip protector: A piece of rubber or other material designed to protect the lower tip of the bow and hold the string loop in place.

Bow window: The cut-out section above the grip in a bow; also called sight window.

Bowyer: A bow designer and maker.

Brace height: The best distance, as recommended by the manufacturer, from the throat of the handle to the string, which will result in the best performance of your bow. Also known as "string height."

Bracing: To string a bow; to bring a bow to proper tension for shooting by placing loops of bowstring into the bow nocks at each limb tip.

Broadhead: A triangular, sharp, pointed metal arrowhead used for hunting.

Brush button: A soft rubber object near each end of the bowstring to prevent brush from catching in juncture of limb and bowstring. Also acts as a string silencer.

Butt: Backstop for arrows—target, matt.

Cam bow: Compound bow with egg-shaped eccentrics instead of round eccentrics.

Cant: Tilting bow right or left while shooting.

Cast: Distance and speed a bow shoots an arrow.

Center-shot bow: One in which the arrow rests in the exact center of the cut-out sight window rather than toward the side.

Clicker: A metal device attached to side of bow above or below the arrow rest that acts as a draw check and trigger for the shot. Arrow is placed under the metal strip and drawn through it. Metal strip clicks against the bow and tells you the arrow has been completely drawn.

Closed stance: Shooting stance in which line to target flows from tip of back foot through ball of front foot to target center.

Clout: Long-distance shooting using a 48-foot target flat on the ground. Color-coded chain is used to mark distances from center. Men shoot from 180 yards, women from 120 or 140 yards.

Cock feather: The odd-colored feather positioned at right angles to the nock. Also known as the index feather.

Composite bow: A bow made of two or more kinds of material, usually wood and fiberglass.

Compound bow: Bow utilizing a cable system with an eccentric pulley at each limb tip; it stores high energy and produces peak resistance at mid-draw and dropoff in resistance beyond this point. The archer thus has a hold weight or anchor weight less than the actual draw weight of the bow.

Creeping: Letting the drawing hand edge forward before or during release.

Crest: Identifying paint markings on the arrow, usually bands close to the fletching.

Dead release: Releasing the string by allowing the string fingers to relax without moving drawing hand back or forward.

Draw: Pulling the bowstring back into full anchor position.

Draw check: Simply determining the amount of arrow drawn for each shot. Also another name for clicker.

Drawing arm: The arm that draws back the bowstring.

Drawing fingers: The index, second, and third fingers of the drawing hand.

Draw length: The length of an arrow needed by an archer, measured at full draw from the back of the bow to the bottom of the slot in the arrow nock.

Draw weight: The energy in pounds required to draw a bow a specified distance (usually 28 inches).

Drift: Natural deflection of an arrow from its intended path due to a crosswind.

Dynabow: Type of compound bow with one cam on lower limb tip and no eccentric on upper limb tip.

Efficiency: In a bow, it is the amount of energy output over the energy input expressed as a percentage.

End: A specified number of arrows shot at one time or position before scoring and retrieving.

Face: The part of the bow facing the shooter. Can also mean a target face.

Field archery: A competitive round shot at various distances and generally laid out in a wooded area to simulate hunting conditions.

Field arrow: An arrow with a long, tapered point, used outdoors for field archery, stump shooting, and roving.

Field captain: Man on the target range in charge of a tournament.

Finger sling: A leather or rope strip with a loop at either end, which permits an archer to hold the bow loosely by inserting his thumb and index fingers of the bow hand into these loops, letting the bow jump against the sling upon release of the shot.

Finger tab: A small piece of leather (or plastic) that protects the drawing fingers and gives a smoother release.

Fletching: Feathers or vanes on an arrow that guide and stabilize the arrow in flight.

Flight: A competitive round of shooting for distance. Also the path of an arrow.

Flight arrow: A long, thin, light arrow, usually barreled with small vanes and point, used in distance shooting.

Flight compensator: Metal object placed under the stabilizers that counteracts any fault causing torque.

Flinch: A sudden body and arm movement caused by indecision or desire to release too early at full draw.

Flu-flu: Spiral or extra-large fletching on an arrow used for wing shooting because the extra wind drag, though allowing normal fast flight for a few yards, soon slows the arrow (usually within 50-60 yards).

Follow-through: Holding the release position to insure direction and accurate flight of the arrow.

Free style: Shooting with the aid of a bow sight and other accuracy aids.

Freezing: Early stage of target panic. Archer comes to full draw and anchors with the sight outside the bull's-eye. His form freezes there and he is unable to move the sight onto the gold.

Glove: A covering worn (usually by hunters) to protect the drawing fingers from the string.

Gold: Center of the target.

Grain: Unit used in weighting arrows.

Grip: That part of the bow handle where the bow hand is placed.

Ground quiver: A rod of metal stuck into the ground, shaped to hold arrows and bows for the archer on the range.

Grouping: A cluster or strike pattern of arrows that have been shot.

Handle riser: The center part of the bow, exclusive of the limbs.

Hanging arrow: An arrow that has penetrated the target with the tip only and hangs down across the target face.

Head: The tip, point, or pile of the arrow.

Helical: Fletch placement that places fletch at slight offset from straight and also places a slight curvature in the fletching from back to front.

Hen feathers: The two feathers that lie next to the string; usually the same color, but different from the cock feather.

High wrist: Top of wrist held in line with top of bow arm; pressure flows through V of thumb and forefinger and bones of hand, then into wrist. More tension is placed on wrist muscles than in other wrist positions.

Holding: Holding an arrow at full draw while aiming.

Index: The raised piece of plastic on the nock of an arrow that is in line with the cock feather.

Instability: In a bow, exaggerates small errors of form, causing them to become major faults. Usually the unstable bow is a result of a poor combination of design features.

Instinctive shooting: Aiming and shooting arrows without using the pre-gap or point-of-aim methods or a bowsight. Usually more learned than purely instinctive, and is called ''bare bow'' shooting.

Jerking: Pulling the drawing hand sharply backward or down as the arrow is released.

Jig: A device for putting feathers on the arrow. Same label is given to the device that makes strings.

Kick: Recoil or jarring of the bow upon release.

Kinetic energy: The product of force over a distance of action, producing a motion that, without friction, is called kinetic energy.

Kisser button: Device attached to the string that contacts the lips when they and head angle are in the correct anchor position, furnishing an additional contact point to insure consistency of draw and anchor.

Lady paramount: Woman in charge of a tournament.

Laminated: Refers to a number of pieces of material bonded together to take advantage of the best features of each different variety.

Level: A small fluid level attached to the bow that aids the archer in maintaining a vertical bow position.

Limbs: The working portions of the bow above and below the handle-riser section.

Live release: Release style that allows drawing hand to slide back along side of neck in follow-through. Also called the flying release.

Longbow: A bow with no recurve.

Loop: The woven or served bend in the ends of a bowstring that fit into the limb notches when the bow is braced. Also called the eye.

Loose: Old term meaning the act of releasing the string.

Low wrist: Hand is placed flat against bow handle, with pressure flowing directly into forearm bone.

Mass weight: The actual, physical weight of the bow.

Match: A competitive event, usually by mail.

Midnock: A nock tapered down from the base to the groove, giving a smoother release.

Mis-nock: The arrow falls out of the bow on release instead of flying to the target. This occurs when the string is not in the nock of the arrow at release.

NAA: National Archery Association, the internationally recognized body for amateur archery in the United States.

NFAA: National Field Archery Association.

Nock: (1) The grooved plastic unit at the back end of the arrow into which the string is placed. (2) The technique of placing the arrow on the bowstring. (3) The grooves at each limb tip that hold the bowstring in position.

Nocking point: A specific location on the string where the arrow is nocked for each shot.

Nocking point height: When you properly nock your arrow, the distance it is placed above square (or 90°) on the string.

Nock locator: The stop on the string against which the arrow nock is placed when properly nocked.

Open stance: A foot position on the shooting line in which the line to the target runs from the instep of the right foot to the toe of the left foot to the target center.

Overbowed: Using a bow heavier than you can draw, hold, and *shoot* accurately for a continued length of time.

Overdraw: In reference to the arrow, to draw so far that the point passes the face of the bow; in reference to the bow, to draw beyond its maximum safe distance.

Overshoot: To shoot above and beyond the target.

Overstrung: String is too short for bow, string height is thus too great.

Pass-through: Arrow goes completely through the target. Because of difficulty in actual scoring of such an arrow, a predetermined scoring value is usually applied for pass-throughs.

Peeking: Tilting head to right or left of string to look at the arrow in flight. Hinders good scoring.

Peep sight: A small aperture placed in the string that lines up with the aiming eye and acts as a rear sight.

Pinching: Squeezing the nock of the arrow during the draw.

Pinch nock: Nock with narrow slot that widens into a circle at base of slot. Snaps lightly on bowstring and prevents arrow from falling off string.

Pin sight: A type of bowsight that makes use of the head of a pin or some facsimile, such as a small dot, etc.

Pivot point: That spot on the grip that is farthest from the string when the bow is braced.

Plucking: Pulling the release hand perpendicularly away from the face or jawbone upon release.

Point: Forward arrow tip.

Point-blank range: The only distance from the target at which the point-of-aim (using arrow tip as sight) is right on the target center.

Point-of-aim: A method of aiming using a point, usually in front of and below the target, with which the point of the arrow is aligned. Rarely used.

Post sight: A type of bowsight that makes use of a device that projects at a right angle downward or upward, from the mount, the tip of which is lined up with the aiming spot on the target face.

Potential energy: The loading of an elastic object, which stores the energy applied to it. When stored, this energy is said to be potential energy.

Pre-gap (Predraw gap): A method of aiming without a sight, which involves establishment of proper distance from target center to arrow tip when bow arm/shoulder unit is raised but before draw is begun.

Pressure point: That spot on the arrow plate against which the arrow is pushed at the instant of release.

Prism: A sighting device that refracts the sight line, giving a clear view of the target. Available in various degrees of refraction.

Pull: Act of removing arrows from the target. Often also means same as "draw."

Pushing the bow: The act of moving the bow toward and usually to the right side of the target during the act of releasing and following through.

Quiver: Any device to hold arrows—ground, hip, back, or bow.

Range: (1) Distance to be shot. (2) The place where shooting takes place.

Range finder: A device to aid the archer in relocating the position of his aiming point.

Rebound: An arrow that hits the scoring face and bounces back toward archer.

Recurve: A bow that curves forward at the limb tips.

Reflexed bow: A bow that bends backward in its entirety when unstrung, but does not necessarily have recurved ends. Bows may be recurved and reflexed.

Release: Allowing the string to roll off the fingers from full draw and propel the arrow.

Ring sight: Circular hood is used, with internal pin removed, to sight on target. Hood is aligned with the appropriate scoring circle and proper aiming is achieved.

Riser: The center part of the bow that includes the handle but not the limbs.

Round: A specified number of ends at a specified distance or distances and target sizes.

Roving: Shooting at random targets such as stumps, paper, clumps of grass, and so on, with unknown and varying distances; good practice for hunting.

Scoring area: That part of the target face made up of the scoring circles.

Self: Bow or arrow made from a single piece of wood.

Serving: The thread wrapping on the center of the bowstring and on the loops to prevent fraying and add strength.

Setup: The preparation of your tackle to achieve its top potential.

Shaft: (1) The main portion of the arrow. (2) An unfinished base component of an arrow.

Shelf: The horizontal, or base, segment of the sight window cutout. With a rug, also serves as arrow rest.

Shooting line: Line parallel to targets, and a specific distance away, from which all archers shoot.

Sight window: That part of the upper limb just above the grip that has been cut away to allow the arrow to rest closer to the center of the bow.

Sinking: The gradual loss of a bow's power.

Six golds: A perfect end on the International target face.

Snake: Act of an arrow disappearing under the grass.

Snap shooting: The act of releasing the arrow as soon as the bowsight lines up with any part of the gold on the target face, or as soon as the string touches the proper anchor during the draw.

Solid bow: Common reference to a bow made entirely of fiberglass or plastics.

Speednock: One that has a molded index on top of the nock to locate the cock feather by feel.

Spine: The strength and flexibility of the arrow, which must match the thrusting power (draw weight) of the bow.

Spiral: The angled position fletching occupies on the shaft.

Spot: The aiming center of a target face.

Square stance: A foot position on the shooting line in which the line to the target runs from the toes of the right foot to the toes of the left foot to the target center.

Stability: The ability of a bow to absorb small errors of form by its own design factors.

Stabilizer: Additional weights extending in front of and at each end of riser, which help to eliminate torque and absorb the shock of the release.

Stacking: The rapid and disproportionate increase of limb resistance during the last few inches of draw.

String: (1) Bowstring. (2) Act of placing limbs under tension by hooking loops in notches at each limb tip.

String fingers: The fingers (usually three) used to draw back the bowstring.

String height: The distance between the throat of the bow handle and the bowstring. Same as brace height.

String notch: The grooves near the tip of each limb into which the loops of the bowstring fit when the bow is braced.

Strung bow: A bow ready to shoot.

Tackle: The equipment used by an archer.

Target: The grass, straw, excelsior, or other backing to which the target face is attached.

Target arrow: A lightweight arrow with a target point.

Target captain: In a tournament, the person at each target designated to call the value of, and pull the arrows for, all the archers at that target.

Target face: Scoring area.

Target panic: Inability to place and hold the sight in the center of the target and release without disturbing the aiming alignment.

Throwing: Moving the bow hand to the left (right-handed archer) upon release.

Tiller: When both limbs of a bow are balanced in performance, one to the other, and correctly aligned throughout the limb and recurves.

Tip: The outermost end of the upper and lower limbs of the bow.

Torque (negative): A rotation or twisting action anticlockwise of the bow handle (to the right for a right-handed archer).

Torque (positive): A rotation or twisting action clockwise of the bow handle (to the left for a right-handed archer).

Toxophilite: A student of archery or an archer.

Trajectory: Path of an arrow in flight.

Tree stand: (1) Position taken in tree by bowhunter. (2) Portable or permanent device placed in tree for hunter to stand upon.

Tuning: The needed adjustments in your tackle to achieve perfect arrow flight.

Twisted limb: The extreme end of the limb is not in line with the main portion of the bow. Caused by improper bracing or storage.

Underbowed: Using a bow of too light draw weight for the archer.

Understrung bow: A bow having too long a string, resulting in a brace height that is too low for efficient shooting.

Vanes: Fletching made of plastic that are weather- and wind-proof.

Wand: A narrow stick used as a target.

Wand shooting: Shooting at a slat two inches wide and six feet high from a long distance.

Windage: Left-right correction in sight setting to allow for arrow drift in the wind.

Wobble: Erratic movement of a flying arrow.

Wrist sling: A device of string, leather, or other material, attached to the bow below the grip, then looped over the archer's wrist. This makes it possible to keep the bowhand fingers relaxed, because it prevents the bow from falling to the ground during release and follow-through. Also called a bow sling.